THE PAPERBACK FANATIC

Issue 42

Published November 2019

FANATICAL THOUGHTS

Welcome to issue 42 of **The Paperback Fanatic**.

This issue is something of a gathering of writers and editors who are documenting the paperback (and related) culture of the 1960s and 70s. I find it especially heartening that so many good books are being generated by a shared passion for the same types of media that I celebrate in these pages. The sheer scope and breadth of their works is proof that we are collectively drawing on a well that is both deep and diverse.

All are professional, whereas am I strictly an amateur, so they don't require my approval or coverage, but I am very pleased to feature them in these pages and hopefully do my bit to publicise their works to an interested audience. But these are not glorified promotion pieces and I am confident that you will gain some new insights from their thinking. For instance, Richard Perez Seves on how fetish-art is viewed by the mainstream and S M Guariento's impassioned defence of the movie tie-in paperback.

Issue 43 of **The Fanatic** is a Gold Medal Special and will probably be ready to go to print by the time you read this. Next off the blocks is the all-reviews special of **Pulp Horror**, which is shaping up to be 100 reviews of vintage paperbacks and will be out in Spring 2020. It will be followed up by a **Hot Lead** all-reviews special. And a second issue of **Monster Maniacs** will follow and a secret project which I'm very excited about. 2020 is going to be busy! I've also contributed a chapter on vintage paperbacks to a proper, grown-up, professional book, which will be out Halloween next year.

I hope you enjoy this issue. I plan to attend the UK paperback fair on November 24th and will pen a report for issue 43.

Best wishes.

Justin.

Issue 42
Published November 2019
Edited by Justin Marriott
Assistant Editor Jim O'Brien
Proof read by Tom Tesarek

Special thanks to all of this issue's contributors.
Scott Carlson, Bill Cunningham, James Doig, S M Guariento, Andrew Nette, Richard Pérez Seves, Nigel Taylor and Darrin Venticinque

Correspondence welcome but I wouldn't want to distract you from that porcupine eating corn-on-the-cob clip on You Tube
thepaperbackfanatic@sky.com

FANATICAL CONTENTS

A NEW PEAK IN HORROR
Darrin Venticinque reveals the secret cover art for cult horror Eat Them Alive. Page 4

THE DEVIL IS A GENTLEMAN
James Doig conjures up correspondence between legendary collector Graeme Flanagan and Britain's occult author Dennis Wheatley. Page 8

DARK FORCES AT WORK
The Fanatic uses dark forces rather than a correct address to go book-shopping. Page 12

THE VOYAGE OF CARLSON
Scott Carlson recreates the film Bullitt, but with a trunk/boot (delete as applicable) of sleaze paperbacks. Page 16

YOUNG, SHARKEY AND WILSON
Nigel Taylor forms a quartet with three lesser-known SF authors. Page 26

TRIPPING THE INK FANTASTIC
S M Guariento talks about *Light Into Ink* his new book on movie tie-ins. Page 36

STANTON UNMASKED
Richard Perez Pérez whips The Fanatic into shape on the importance of fetish art and his book on Eric Stanton. Page 46

THE MAD PULP BASTARD
Bill Cunningham escapes from his straight-jacket to talk about his mission to preserve some of pulp culture's finest. Page 56

STICKING IT TO THE MAN
Andrew Nette continues to revolutionise the study of paperbacks with his latest. Page 64

DARRIN VENTICINQUE solves the mystery surrounding the art for the UK edition of the notorious Eat Them Alive. Aided and abetted by JANE FRANK.

A NEW PEAK IN HORROR!

Eat Them Alive is the giant mantis nasty paperback whose cult reputation and price has increased in the four decades since its first printing. Recently a German language edition – probably unauthorised – in a hardback limited edition of 999 copies was published. Readers have often speculated as to the underwhelming packaging of the UK New English Library edition which looked like a detail of a larger painting. Thanks to the generosity of Darrin Venticinque, a long-term supporter of The Paperback Fanatic and premier collector of horror paperback art, and also premier art dealer Jane Frank of Worlds of Wonder, the truth can be told – and seen!

The following are reproduced from e-mails sent by Darrin and Jane.

Darrin - Well, several years ago I was invited to visit the home of Jane & Howard Frank, who had a collection so big and valuable that they published 2 coffee-table sized books which featured it!

After hours of viewing their exhibit (since there was no other way to describe it), I made it to Janes' favourite part of the house, which she dubbed "The Bug Hall". Basically, if the painting featured a bug in it, it was hung in that hallway. One other painting, for example, that was in the hallway was Steve Crisps' art to **Pan Book of Horrors #26** (I'm sure you know the book).

So, I'm looking at the paintings and I run across "the praying mantis piece". At first I did not pay it much attention since I did not recognize it from any book... and who would! I thought it was just some private commission. It wasn't until I finished the hallway portion of my trip (and it was a big hallway) that I decided to go back and have another look at it. After further examining I thought that it looked vaguely familiar... then it just HIT ME and I freaked out! I was like "Jane ! You have *Eat Them Alive?*" She didn't know what I was talking about. After explaining it further to her, this is the story she told me (however, before I tell her story, let me inform you that she

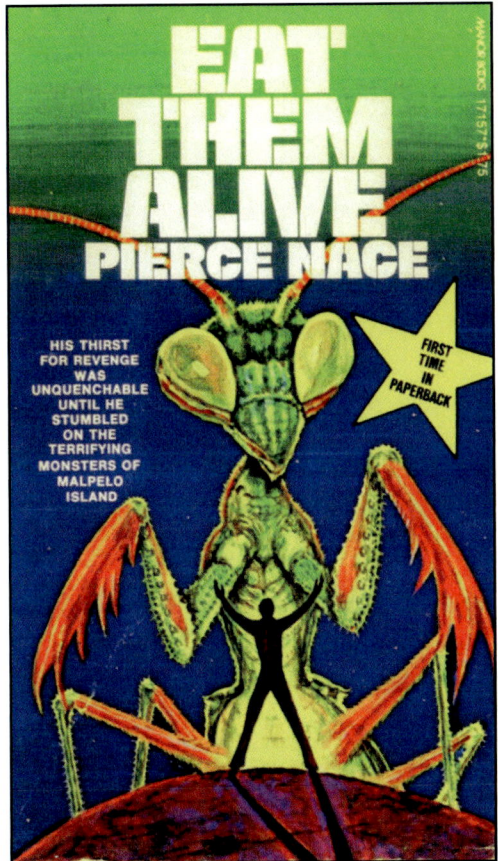

1977 US edition from Manor Books which is likely to have been the first edition.

1977 UK reprint by New English Library, which carried a piece of art which had obviously been cropped.

was, and still is, a selling agent for artists who have works to be sold but do not want any involvement in the process of the sale. They want her to do all the work and take a commission for her effort, then send the rest of the money to their bank accounts).

So, Jane basically tells me that at the time (however many years ago; it was quite a while), she was selling art for Tim White. He was sending her stuff, she was selling it. At one point during their "business partnership" she asks him if he has any paintings with bugs or the like in them, for her own collection. This painting came up in the conversation, but he did not want to send it to her since he was so angry about the way New English Library reproduced it that he did not want it even mentioned in conversation (or so that is how I interpreted her story). He did not even sign it; basically disowning it due to its fate on the book cover. From what I remember, she did much pleading, etc. to get it from him, not even knowing the book cover it was on. Eventually he sent it to her with other paintings and the rest is history. She said Tim is a tough person to deal with and no longer sells for him. His website is not even active any longer. When I did write to him, he never responded.

A few years later, The Frank Collection was being substantially down-sized via sales to customers and to the Heritage Auction house. They were moving to a much smaller place and it was time to start selling-off. I was not aware of this until we spoke on the phone one day and she mentioned it all to me. She

A photo from Darrin of the full painting in its frame.

remembered my fondness / reaction to *Eat Them Alive*, so offered to sell it to me, in addition to the Steve Crisp piece and the Terry Oakes painting to *Locusts* by Guy N. Smith (I'm sure you know that one as well). After some negotiating, we came to an agreed-upon price for the 3 paintings and I had them less than a week later.

Jane Frank- I remember my relationship with Tim White very clearly, "as if" it were yesterday. Oddly I also kept most of my emails with him, among them ones relating to *Eat them Alive*. The lack of a signature on many of Tim's paintings (not just this one), when I started representing him, was only one of many subjects prompting back-and-forth discussion. What Darrin may not know (because the piece was framed when he bought it) is that IT IS actually signed. Here is an excerpt from Tim's email, back in 2001 regarding how that came to be....

(Tim) I am prepared to sign my work inside the image for paintings you sell for me if it is so important. But the signature would be small. I will sign the margin as always and the back too. I hope that you will find this satisfactory.
Kr, - T
   p.s. *Eat Them Alive* will remain signed in the margin though! I could always sneeze on it instead of signing it! Signed by DNA!! I could send you a toe-nail clipping for authenticity..!!

As the above suggests, we definitely disagreed on the need for signing "in clear view" - and although I won that round, it was only a prelude to the many areas for conflict that followed, all of them based on some departure or another from standard artistic or agent/client practice (just like this one). I believe my words to him at the time, ones that would remain the same today, "if you are alive and able to wiggle your fingers (or toes), collectors expect to see your works signed."

So, there you have it. The truth behind the image that appeared on the paperback of one of the most baffling and unusual cult items of recent times.

   Special thanks to Darrin and Jane.

A close-up of the photo provided by Darrin showing the original in all of its gory glory. The decapitation of the natives on the island on which the mantises emerge, as well as the mist are all accurate to the book.

JAMES DOIG shares two letters written to his late great friend and collector Graeme Flanagan from the famous occult author Dennis Wheatley

THE DEVIL IS A GENTLEMAN

In 1967, as a nineteen year-old, Graeme Flanagan, who was to become a respected Australian book collector and bibliographer, wrote to his literary idol at that time, Dennis Wheatley. As Phil Baker points out the introduction to his biography of Wheatley, *The Devil is a Gentleman***, Wheatley had moved from being "Public Thriller Writer No.1" in the 1930s and "Prince of Thriller Writers" in the 1940s to becoming Britain's "occult uncle" in the '60s and '70s.**

Although Graeme had read and enjoyed almost all of Wheatley's books, it was clear his main interest was his occult novels. These were easily obtainable in Australia in Arrow's cheap, yellow-spined paperback editions.

Perhaps true to his character as an English gentleman, Wheatley responded personally to letters from fans and Graeme was no exception. Reproduced and transcribed here are two letters Graeme received from Wheatley in January and November 1967. They were written within a few days of receiving Graeme's letters and shed some light on Wheatley's interests: the occult, the films that were being made of his work, and his forthcoming books.

The unnamed musician in the first letter is the English composer Eugene Goossens, whose association with Rosaleen Norton, the so called "Witch of Kings Cross", caused a scandal in the 1950s. Goossens was forced to leave Australia in disgrace when police searched his bags after his arrival at Sydney airport in March 1956 and found photographs, books and other items that were considered obscene under Australian law. Norton was a notorious artist and occultist who practiced magical ceremonies and was regularly in the news for her activities. An exhibition of her art at Melbourne University was raided by the police and four paintings were removed as obscene.

Later in life Graeme Flanagan was a keen correspondent with other writers who became good friends, including Robert Bloch, J. Vernon Shea, Fritz Leiber, Margaret St Clair and Basil Wells.

7th January, 1967
Dear Mr Flanagan

Very many thanks for your letter of the 1st January. It is always a pleasure to hear from readers of my books, and particularly from one like yourself who has read so many of them.

I note your particular interest in those of my books with occult backgrounds and I can assure you that I have reason to believe that black magic is still practiced in all the great cities of the world today, as well as by native races such as the Mau-Mau and the Indians of Brazil.

With regards to Australia, if you care to make enquiries among your friends, one or other will probably be able to tell you the name of the famous musician, (I cannot, for obvious reasons, give you his name myself), who, a few years ago was arrested while entering Australia and, among whose luggage there was found all the ceremonial paraphernalia of a Satanist. He was not, however, charged with being a black magician, as I think there are no laws against witchcraft today, but he was charged and convicted of having in his possession a quantity of pornographic literature.

With regard to my writing. I write only one book a year and my next is not due to come out until August. Its background is Mexico at the present day, but it also contains a great deal about the ancient civilization, as I bring reincarnation into the story.

With kindest thoughts.

LYMINGTON 3115.

DENNIS WHEATLEY.
GROVE PLACE.
LYMINGTON, HANTS.

Please add to address: SO4.9RA.

Graeme Flanagan, Esq.,   13th November,
61, Caley Crescent,   1967
Narrabundah,
CANBERRA, A.C.T.2604,
Australia.

Dear Mr. Flanagan,

    Many thanks for your letter of the 6th November. It is always a pleasure to hear from readers who have enjoyed my books, and especially from someone like yourself who has collected all of them, with the exception of SATURDAYS WITH BRICKS.

    As every one of my books is still in print, you can obtain a copy of this book by writing to the publishers:

    Messrs. Hutchinson Limited,
        178/202, Great Portland Street,
            London, W.1.

    It is true that the Duke de Richleau died at the end of DANGEROUS INHERITANCE. He was over eighty-five, and had lived a very full and interesting life; but there are many gaps in his younger days which I intend to fill, so you may be sure that there will be more books about his adventures

    THE FORBIDDEN TERRITORY was the first book of mine to be published. This was in 1933, and it was then reprinted seven times
                    /in....

 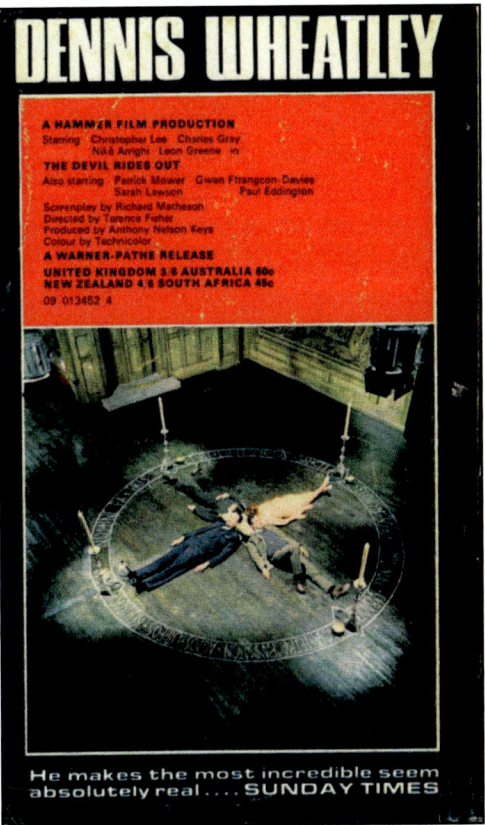

The Arrow 1966 movie tie-in to The Devil Rides Out, which Dennis Wheatley references in his letter to Graeme Flanagan

13 November 1967
Dear Mr Flanagan,

Many thanks for your letter of the 6th November. It is always a pleasure to hear from readers who have enjoyed my books, and especially from someone like yourself who has collected all of them, with the exception of *Saturdays With Bricks*.

As every one of my books is still in print, you can obtain a copy of this book by writing to the publishers.

It is true that the Duke de Richeleau died at the end of *Dangerous Inheritance*. He was over eighty-five, and had lived a very full and interesting life; but there are many gaps in his younger days which I intend to fill, so you may sure that there will be more books about his adventures.

The Forbidden Territory was the first book of mine to be published. This was in 1933, and it was reprinted seven times in seven weeks. It was also filmed, as was *the Eunuch of Stamboul*, way back in the 1930s.

At the moment, I have two books of mine being filmed at the same time in this country – *The Devil Rides Out* and *Uncharted Seas*. The latter will be released under the title of *The Lost Continent*. These two films are having a world-wide release, so I hope that when they arrive in Australia you will enjoy them, as both of them are remarkably true to the original story.

I have pleasure in enclosing the two cards you sent me, duly autographed.

    Yours sincerely
    Dennis Wheatley

A gallery of photo-covers for Dennis Wheatley's occult novels which appeared on Arrow Books paperbacks in the mid 1970s.

DARK FORCES AT WORK

In the 1990s I planned my first visit to Hay-on-Wye, the famous "town of books". However, I accidentally drove to Ross-on-Wye, the not so famous town of charity (thrift) shops. Before I realised my mistake, I did buy these seven Dennis Wheatley paperbacks from a charity shop, presumably dumped by some raving Satanist retiring from all of that goat-stuff.

A lost traveller discovering arcane occult volumes in a remote town…. Coincidence, or a conspiracy of the type of dark forces Wheatley warned gullible readers about? Me making a stupid mistake in choosing my destination, which Tourist Information at Ross-on-Wye assured me happens all of the time and take one of these photo-copied pages showing direction how to get to Hay-on-Wye from here?

You make your mind up. Whatever, the Wheatley letters gave me a great excuse to reproduce these photo-covers……

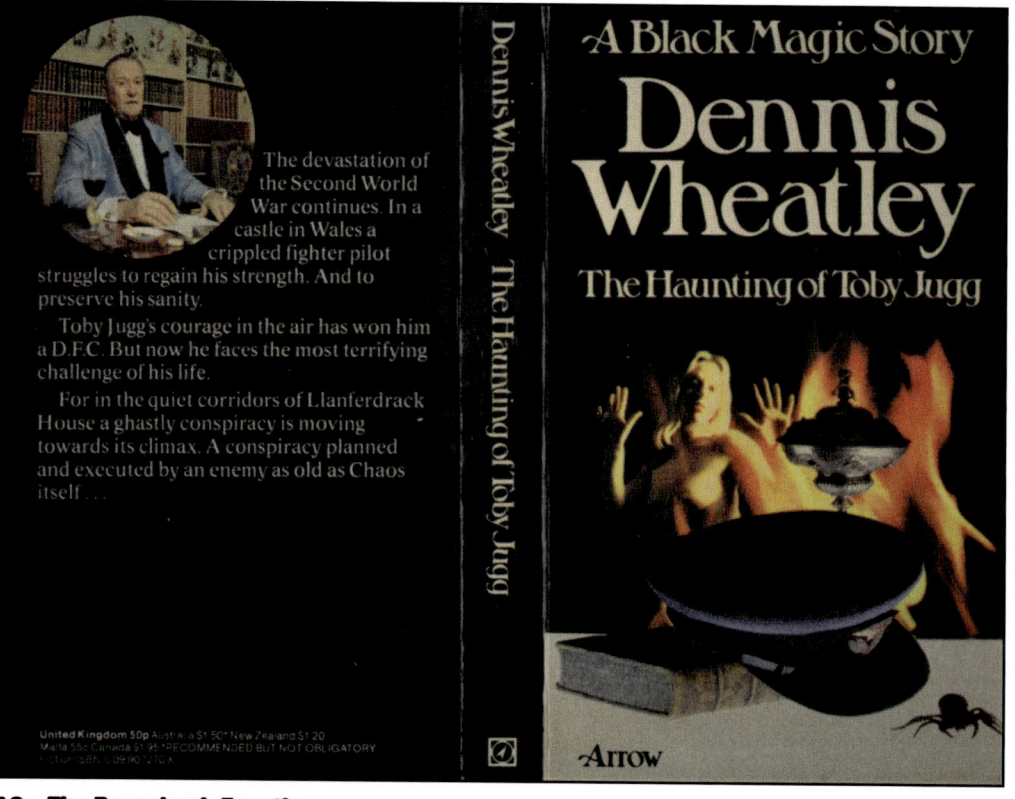

A Black Magic Story
Dennis Wheatley
They Used Dark Forces

It is 1943. Gregory Sallust parachutes into Nazi Germany. His mission – to penetrate the secret rocket installations at Peenemünde.

Intelligence reports have spoken of contacts on the ground, war-weary Germans anxious to hasten the end of hostilities. But nothing has prepared him for Ibrahim Malacou: hypnotist, astrologer and disciple of Satan.

For both men this is only the start of a long, uneasy partnership. And the first in a chain of events that will lead Gregory into the most desperate gamble of his life...

United Kingdom 50p Australia $1.50* New Zealand $1.20
Malta 55c Canada $1.95 *RECOMMENDED BUT NOT OBLIGATORY
Fiction ISBN 0 09 907260 2

Arrow

A Black Magic Story
Dennis Wheatley
The Devil Rides Out

When the Duke de Richleau and Rex van Ryn sat at dinner that night, there was only one topic of conversation: what lay behind the disappearance of Simon Aron from his usual haunts?

The answer was more terrible than they feared. Their oldest and dearest friend had fallen prey to Satanism – the deadliest enemy of mankind.

If de Richleau and Rex were to save him, they had first to conquer the Forces of Darkness. And that meant treading the most perilous path of all...

United Kingdom 45p Australia $1.40* New Zealand $1.05
Malta 50c Canada $1.75 *RECOMMENDED BUT NOT OBLIGATORY
Fiction ISBN 0 09 907240 8

Arrow

A Black Magic Story

Dennis Wheatley
Strange Conflict

1940. The sky over London fills with the drone of German bombers on their mighty mission of death. But in the darkened streets below the Duke de Richleau wrestles with a still more pressing problem.

Britain's Atlantic convoys are her lifeblood. Now an astonishing run of enemy successes threatens to cut off the flow completely. How are the Nazis getting their information?

The Duke de Richleau senses where the truth must lie: on the Astral Plane. Only the foolish – or the very brave – risk their soul and sanity there... but he determines to do so.

Arrow

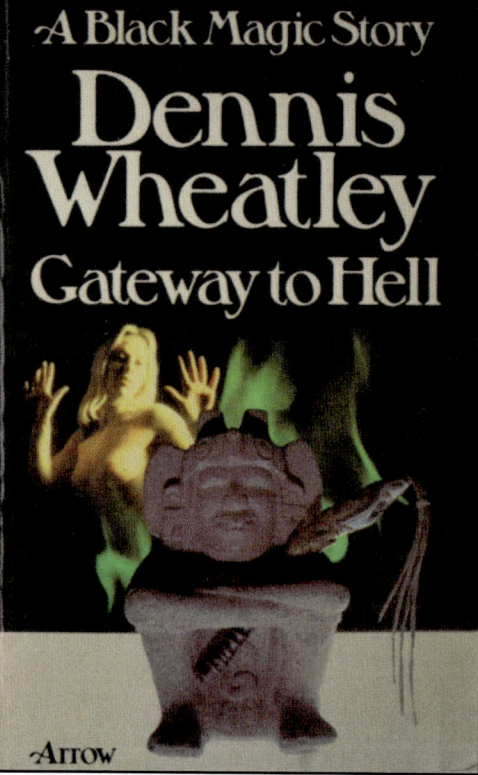

A Black Magic Story

Dennis Wheatley
Gateway to Hell

The Duke de Richleau and his friends had faced many dangers in Russia, Spain and Nazi Germany. Now a new and unexpected menace confronts them: the fourth, Rex van Ryn is missing – and he has made off with more than a million dollars from the Buenos Aires branch of his family bank.

Behind the conventional courtesy of Argentinian society lies a conspiracy of terror and silence – and a trail that leads straight to the Devil himself...

Arrow

Christina seemed no different from any other young girl: polite, attractive and a little shy.

But each evening, as darkness fell, the demonic Power within her betrayed its presence. And a terrible pattern of Evil began to emerge.

Miles away, in the mist and rain of the Essex marshes, a satanic priest has created a hideous creature. Now it was waiting beneath the ancient stones of Bentford Priory for the virgin sacrifice that would give it life...

A Black Magic Story
Dennis Wheatley
To the Devil-a Daughter

Arrow

For years Colonel Verney had suspected a link between Devil-worship and the subversive influence of Soviet Russia. When they found Teddy Morden's crucified body, he knew his grimmest fears were justified.

Then came the Khune affair. And suddenly not only Britain's security but the peace of the world was in danger.

In the course of their duties all of Verney's agents faced possible torture or death. But for Mary the fight against her husband's killers meant danger of a different kind – her total submission to their vicious and degrading rituals...

A Black Magic Story
Dennis Wheatley
The Satanist

Arrow

SCOTT CARLSON sets sail on a cruise of the used book stores of America, reporting back to readers of The Fanatic with tall tales and fishy goings-on.

VOYAGE OF THE CARLSON

I tend not to receive too many requests for articles, but generally when I do it's for more personal pieces, particularly around other collector's experiences of book-hunting on the road. I don't have any articles, but I do have a couple of personal e-mails from Scott Carlson on recent book expeditions, which were really aimed for an audience of myself and his great friend Tom Tesarek.

They are reprinted below, with Scott's permission and with some of the private jokes removed. When reading it's worth noting that Scott has the driest sense of humour of anyone I know. Although I think there is a serious case of "methinks the lady does protest too much" in his constant snarky comments he makes about the publications of Carousel.

It was a long and hard winter here in Minnesota. First in January it got down to -28 Fahrenheit (-33 Celsius). Then in February we got 40 inches (102 centimeters) of snow. At least I was able to get out of state in March. I went to Arizona again to visit my mother. And it just so happened that this was over the same weekend as the LA paperback show. What a coincidence. Since Phoenix and Los Angeles are practically next door, I decided to pop over to the show. 4370 miles (7033 kilometers) later I am safe and sound back in Minnesota. I managed to find a couple books along the way, and at the show.

The trip started on Saturday, March 16, at Dreamhaven Books. Greg Ketter was flying out to the show, so I agreed to carry some books out for him. He turned out to have 2 rather large boxes. This turned into a mini-theme of the trip. My sister had bought a large and heavy piece of art last year when she was in Phoenix, too large to take back on the plane. So I carried that back to Minnesota for her. Since my mother is headed back to Minnesota next week, I also carried back a bag of stuff for her. And despite Greg assuring me he would sell most of the books

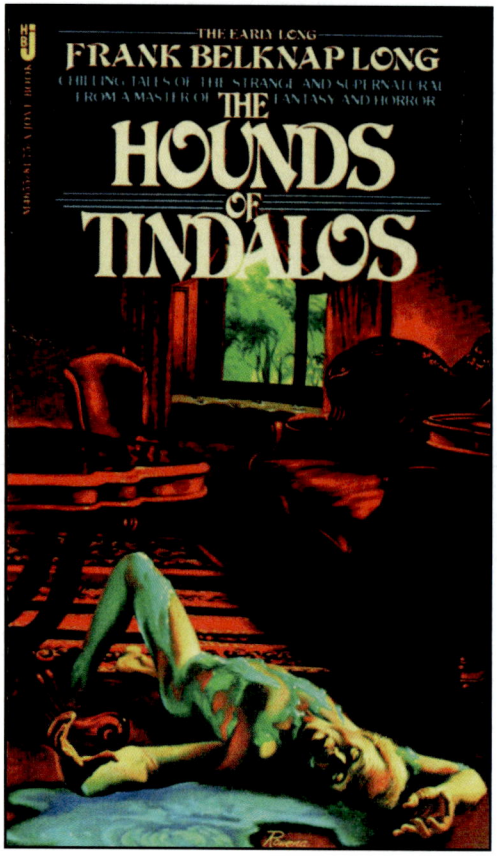

I carried down for him, I ended up carrying back his two large boxes. So my car was cozy on the way back. I left on Sunday. This was a last day of a sale at Half Price Books- I had a 50% off coupon to use, which could be used on one item per store.

I did not find anything at the location in Des Moines - they think that vintage paperbacks are very valuable, way too expensive for me even at 50% off. I managed to find something to buy at two of the Kansas City locations, and at the Wichita location. The Wichita store is new (since I was last in Wichita). But despite this they had a lot of older stuff, and some fairly obscure paperbacks. I found one of the Corgi **Raven** books for Tom. I also found a copy of *Deceived* by Mel White, prominently featured in **The Sleazy Reader 8**. I spent the night at a dump on the east side of Wichita (across the highway from the Half Price).

Bright and early Monday morning I hit the Book-a-Holic on the east side of Wichita. This store was still stuck in the same time warp as the last time I went there. Not surprisingly, a store stuck in a time warp from the seventies didn't have a lot of turnover. I did find a copy of *The Hound of Tindalos* by Frank Belknap Long, the Jove edition with a Rowena cover. I wasn't even aware that this edition existed. Jove did a nice series of **Weird Tales** related paperback during their short existence. It would be nice if someone did an article on these somewhere.

Unfortunately, the time warp over the east side of Wichita doesn't extend to the west side. The two Book-a-Holic locations there were fairly mundane. I found it amusing that one of the Book-a-Holics was next door to a store called "DT's". I didn't stop there. I only managed to find one book between the two. The rest of the day was spent driving to Las

Vegas (New Mexico). Part of this was on a lonely desert road, with no traffic nor signs of humanity. There apparently was a gravitational anomaly here, since something kept pulling the gas pedal to the floor. Fortunately, my car has a limiter and can't go faster than 124 mph (200 kph).

On Tuesday I drove to Santa Fe. This was disappointing. I stopped at a paperback exchange with nothing but new paperbacks, a record and book store with only books I already have, and a "real" bookstore with no paperbacks at all. I did manage to find 4 trade paperbacks at the latter, strictly books I intend to read. I took a quick side trip to Los Alamos to do a bit of spying. I didn't go into the lab proper, since I didn't feel like explaining to the guards the two sealed boxes in the back of my car that I was carrying for a stranger. So I just visited the museum.

After this I drove to Albuquerque. On the way I stopped at Under Charlie's Covers in Bernalillo. This was a great book store. The prices were all over the place, but for the most part were reasonable to cheap. They had many of their older paperbacks bagged at the end of each section, but there was a lot of interesting stuff mixed in the general stock. I found a Ballantine in very good condition that I didn't have - given how many Ballantines I do have, this was no mean feat. I left with half a dozen books.

Albuquerque itself was disappointing, I went back to Downtown Books, but only found a run of the mill Beacon hiding amongst the mysteries. I went to Don's Paperback Exchange. I have read good things about this store, but in fact there was almost nothing older than the nineties in the store. After this I drove on to Holbrook Arizona for the night.

Wednesday I drove to Phoenix, via Payson. Through twisty mountain roads. That pesky gravitational anomaly was still affecting my car, but I was able to fight it off. Since my mother was having a root canal done that morning, instead of going directly to visit her, I hit some bookstores in Phoenix first. The first once was named Books, although it looks like they might also be called Books on 7th Avenue. This was the store where books go to die in Arizona. They had stuff that nobody in their right mind would want to buy.

Fortunately I'm not in my right mind, so I found a few things. Nothing that special, though. It didn't hurt that most paperbacks were $1 to $2. After this I went to Bookmans. While they had some nice titles, I only found one book I needed, one of the absolutely awesome Carousel SF titles.

After this I drove to my mother's place in Apache Junction, so she could beat me in cribbage. Again and again and again. Thursday my mother had some thing she wanted to do in the park, so I hit some bookstores in Mesa and east Phoenix. I tried to hit one in Tempe, but despite what their website said, they were not open. I didn't find that much. I got a copy of *The Male Response* by Brian Aldiss (Panther) and *Expense Account Sinners* by Don Elliott at the Mesa Bookmans. Imagine that, smut like

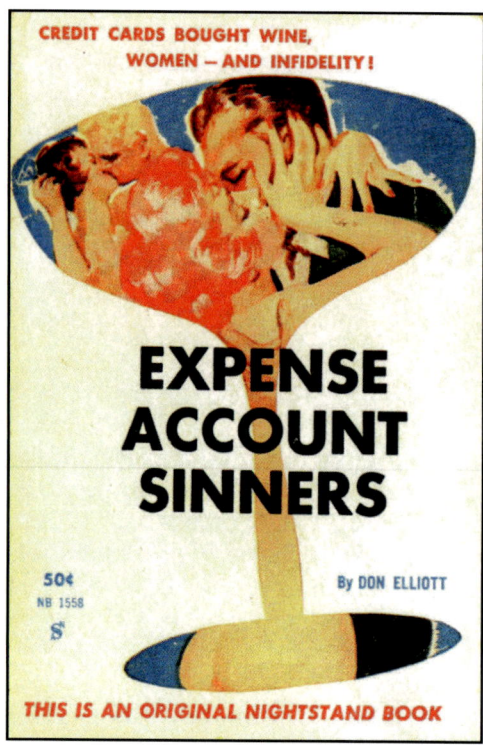

this just sitting on the shelf, where impressionable youth could get their hands on it. I did my part in keeping Mesa clean. The only other thing I got was yet another Carousel SF at Book Gallery in Phoenix.

Book Gallery still had really nice paperbacks, at eye watering prices. But they have moved to the other side of their mini-mall, into a much large space. It was maybe twice as big. They had a lot more general paperbacks. These were priced much more sanely. I would have bought quite a few, if I didn't keep checking my list and seeing that I already had them. On the way out I talked to the owner about the LA paperback show. Apparently he has never been to it, despite Tom Lessor repeated nagging him that he should go.

Technically I did no book shopping on Friday. But I went to a swap meet with my mother, were there were two booths with books. But these were swap meet book, both in quality and condition.

On Saturday I drove to LA. No book shopping at all. I felt the Book DTs coming on. Fortunately there was a remedy for that the next day. I got in too late to go to dinner will Greg and other dealers or get out to Tom Lessor's house. But I met Greg late that night in the parking lot, to give him his boxes of books. Sunday was The Show. I turned down Greg's offer to get there at 7:30 and get in free as his assistant, and instead showed up at 9:00 with the rest of the groundlings. I did a quick first circuit, stopping at promising tables. Then I did a slower circuit, and then an even slower circuit. I was in a middle of a fourth circuit when I left.

On the first circuit I stopped at Jeff Wilmont's table – he had a lot of US and UK SF and horror. I got the Tandem books of horror and ghost stories from him. He said he didn't think they would last very long, and he was right. He sort of chuckled when I asked him if he had any Charles Birkin's. Apparently these are getting hard to find. Art Scott had a table, selling off sleaze he didn't want. I got a stack of Playtime's from him, as well as a New Chariot Library and an All Star with the same cover

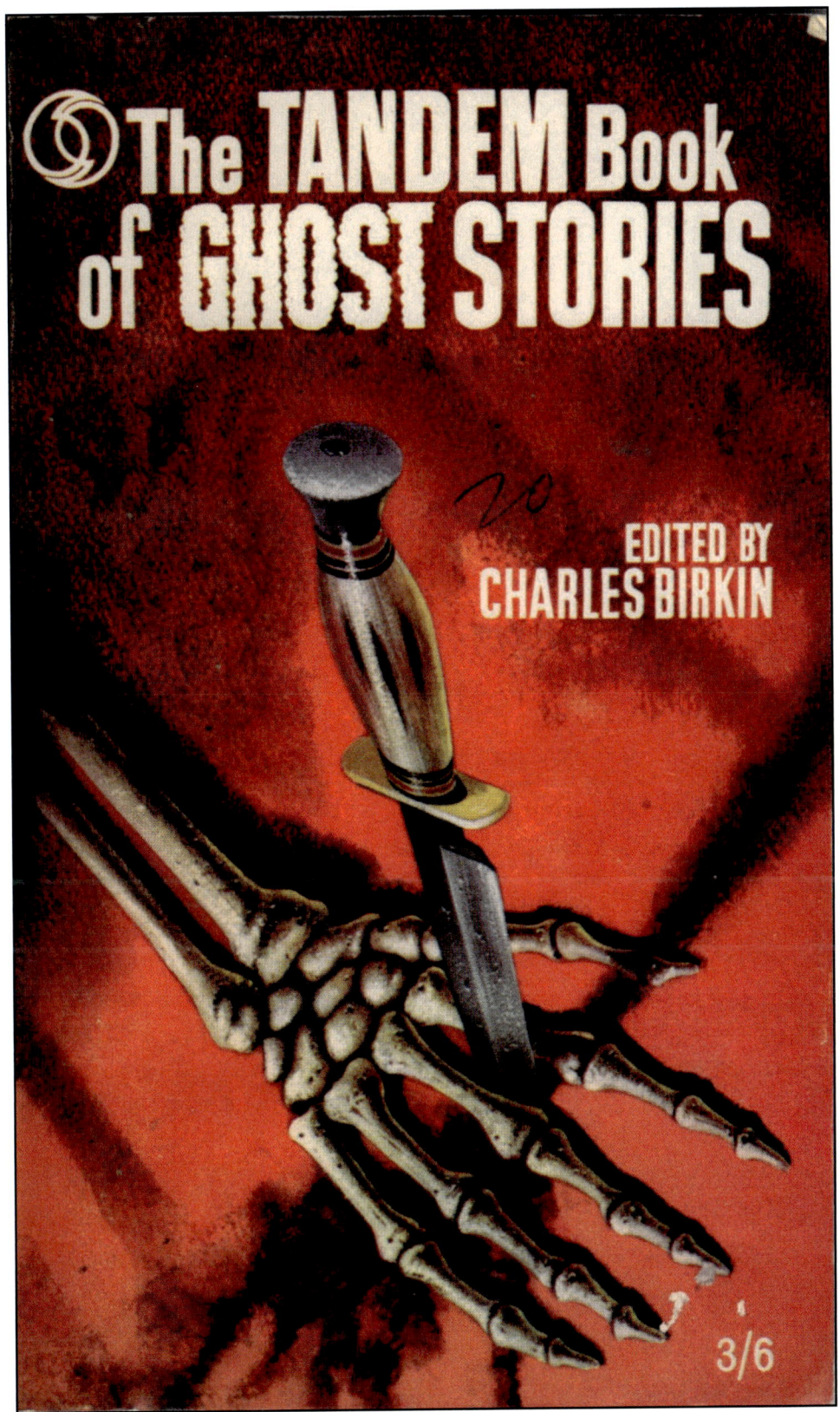

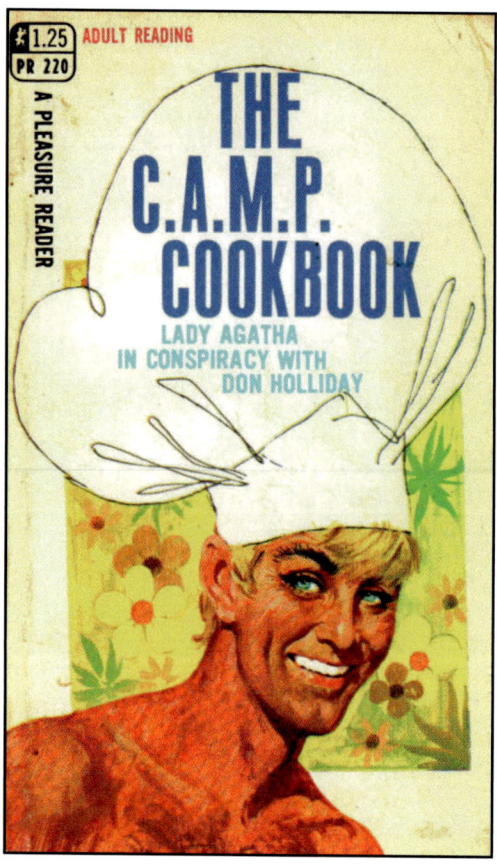

illustration. I also ran into and talked to Bob Speray at his table. Pete Enfantino had a table, right next to Greg's. I got the latest **Digest Enthusiast** from him, as well as 4 issues of **Books Are Everything**. We talked about the **The Sharpshooter** series. I saw Maurice Flanagan of Zardoz Books a few times, but never managed to talk to him.

There were a few other people I should have recognized but couldn't come up with their names. There were a few people who I see at Windy City, but in general it didn't look like there was a lot of overlap. There were a number of tables with local collectors selling off their collections. I got a few books from them. Prices was mostly reasonable, and there were some books that were downright cheap. Lots of people had $1 boxes, and a few of these morphed into 2 for $1 by the end of the day. One of these had a copy of what I believe is the first Challenge Book, *Sea Raiders*, which of course I'd never seen before.

I didn't bring books to have signed, but I bought a signed copy of *Pocketbook Writer* by Charles Nuetzel from the author himself. I was behind a guy in line who had a stack of Powell books to be signed. Kayo Books had a table. They had a complete set of **Man from C.A.M.P.** books. I bought the *C.A.M.P. Cookbook*. I paid a bit too much for it; but he threw in a most interesting hardcover, *Living Hiroshima*, published in 1948 by the Hiroshima Tourist Association. I suspect convincing people to visit Hiroshima in 1948 might have been a hard sell.

Now that I have the *C.A.M.P. Cookbook*, I can start work on my new magazine, which will review sleaze cookbooks. I plan to call it **The Sleazy Eater**. For the cover of the first issue I plan to modify the cover of *The Sin Gang*, which has the arm of a man holding a blowtorch menacing a woman - I plan to have her holding a stick with a wiener on the end over the blowtorch. Or maybe not. This still sounds like a lot of work. And I only have 4 books to review, which will make a pretty slim magazine.

Greg did not have a good show. He did not sell that much, so he packed up a little after three. Since he had two full boxes, I carried them back to Minneapolis. After loading those I took off. I wanted to get out of LA before dark. Other than dodging little old ladies in immaculate cars who drove like they only drove once a week in Pasadena, I had no troubles.

I got as far as St. George Utah that night, and stayed in the nicest hotel of the trip. It is fitting this was St. George, because my map of bookstores simply said "here there be dragons". There is not a lot in this part of Utah, except for twisty mountain roads and 80mph (129 kph) speed limits. On Monday I drove to Denver. I made one stop at a bookstore in Grand Junction Colorado. Other than Westerns it was uninteresting. But they had a great selection of westerns. I got an upgrade of a Ballantine western, and one of the great Carousel westerns. Ah, Colorado. I've never been so high in my life.

At the entrance of the Eisenhower tunnel, at 11,158 feet (3400 meters). Other than that, the Denver area was disappointing. After spending the night at a somewhat scary hotel, I tried to hit bookstores. The one I really wanted to go to, Fahrenheit's, was closed on Tuesdays. I got a couple books as Kilgore's, which was very small but had a lot of interesting SF. I didn't get anything at Colorado's Used Book Store, despite them having a large section of collectable paperbacks. Everything was way, way too expensive. But it was fun listening to the people behind the counter discussing how to price a book that had just come it. It was a crappy UFO book from the 80's, which would not be out of place in a $1 box. Apparently the average price of copies on ABE was $650, which is what the guy looking it up wanted to price it at. The women suggested that $6.50 was more appropriate. I didn't hear the resolution of this discussion, but looking at a few of the (so called) collectable paperback, the average ABE price seems to be the default strategy. They has a sign in the front window saying they weren't currently buying books. No wonder - given their prices, I wonder when was the last time they sold a book.

I left Denver around noon, and drove to Omaha. I managed to get to the Half Price Books there before it closed, and picked up two books. I also proved that I am still not able to drive past a Krispy Kreme doughnuts without stopping.

Wednesday morning I tried to go to the bottom feeder bookstore in Omaha, but again despite what their website said, they were closed. Then I went to Jackson Street Books, in the old market section of Omaha. This is another very good bookstore, in which I have gotten good books in the past. I picked two books out of the display case and two from the general stock. When I brought these to the counter, the guy there looked at them and suggested I look at a box of Internet only books they had. I found one more in there (*Queer Street*, a Lynton Wright Brent Private Edition title).

I spent the rest of Wednesday driving home. I stopped at one final Half Price Books on the way, in Apple Valley Minnesota. And there I found yet another Corgi Raven book. Apparently they are everywhere.

Tom Tesraek and I went to Windy City again this year. We left early to try to beat a snowstorm. We got out of the Twin Cities before it hit. But we drove back into it again half way to Madison, and had terrible roads all the way to Milwaukee, where we stayed the night. To give you some idea of how bad the roads were, we decided to not stop at a bookstore along the way. We only managed to hit a couple Half Prices. But I managed to find a book I'd been looking for quite a while at one of them, *Butchers of Berlin* by Bela von Block. This is a non-sleaze title from Chariot Books.

The next day (Thursday) we drove to the hotel in Chicago. We stopped at a few more Half Prices. We also stopped at Bucket o' Blood books. You would love this store. It is a vaguely horror themed record and book store.

After this we went to Gallery books, where I got the Ace/Audubon *I Spit on your*

Grave by Boris Vian, and the Award/Audubon *The Libertine* by Jacapo Massimo. You would have seen a lot of stuff you wanted at Gallery; but you probably wouldn't have bought that much. Gallery tends to be a bit expensive. We then stopped at Myopic books, but mainly because we were looking for some place to eat. I'm not sure if I've ever bought anything at Myopic. It was the first bookstore on this trip where I didn't buy anything.

Friday was the first day of the show. I picked up a fair amount of sleaze, but nothing that outstanding. The Friday night auction was Robert Weinberg's stuff. There was some very nice stuff, and some very obscure stuff. But there were not that many paperbacks. There were almost no lots I was tempted to bid on. Tom was outbid on a few pulps. Neither of us won anything.

The same mostly held for the Saturday night auction. The first part was Glenn Lord's stuff. I was planning to bid on *Out of Space and Time* by Clark Ashton Smith. But despite what the catalog said, it was signed and inscribed to Glenn Lord from Clark Ashton Smith. That put it out of my price range. The second part of the auction was consignments from convention attendees. Someone put in a copy of the magazine *$1000 Medical Horrors*, a notorious one-shot by Harold Hersey. I really wanted that, and was prepared to pay crazy money for it. Unfortunately (or maybe fortunately?) there were far crazier people in the room. It went for $1300. Gulp.

The drive home Sunday was exciting. Chicago got hit with part 2 of the snowstorm. So roads again were awful again. And once we finally made it out of the snow/slush, we got caught in road construction for an hour.

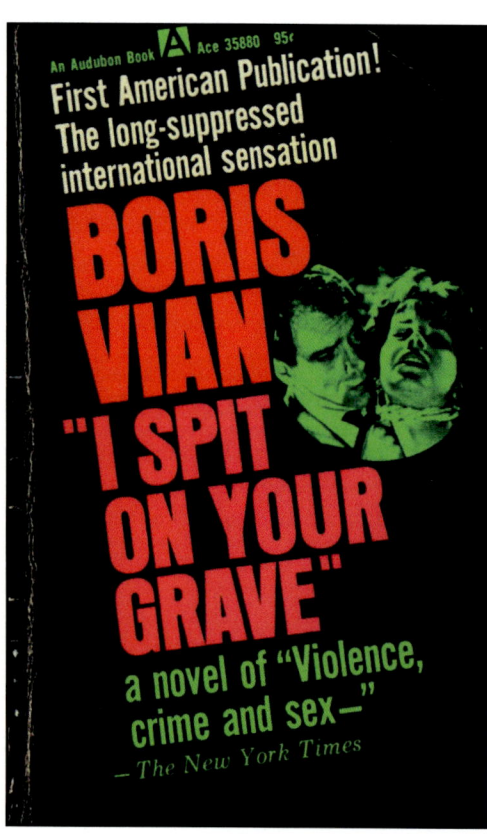

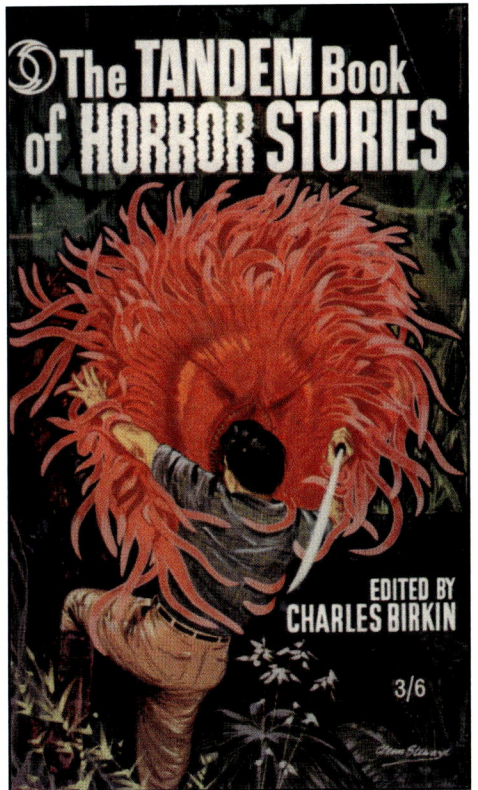
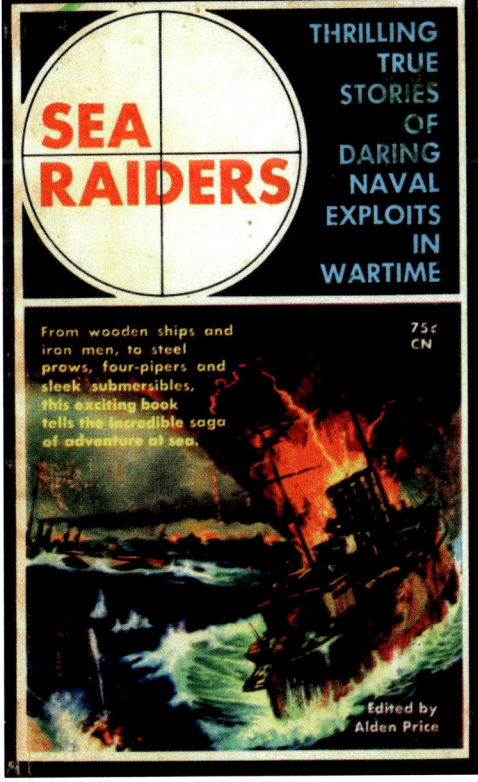

NIGEL TAYLOR returns from visiting Worlds of Strange (his excellent fiction zine) to contribute a profile on the forgotten ones known as-

YOUNG, SHARKEY AND WILSON

There used to be in Jazz Journal, a mag to which my Dad subscribed, a regular column called 'The Forgotten Ones'. At least, I *think* there did – it was a long time ago, and my memory grows faint... Anyway, the purpose of this column was to draw the reader's attention to certain musicians who, once quite famous, had fallen into undeserved obscurity. Jazz and science fiction do not necessarily have much in common (although West Coast trumpeter Shorty Rogers had a minor hit in the 50s with a tune called *Martians, Go Home*. Wonder where he got *that* title?) but it occurred to me that SF too has its share of 'forgotten ones'. In this article I will be putting three of these neglected talents under the microscope. They shared certain qualities – all were perhaps more proficient at the short story form than the novel, all had a gift for humour. They wrote stories that were often whimsical, charming; human stories told in polished prose.

The first of my 'forgotten ones' was deemed sufficiently important in his own lifetime (1915 – 1986) to get his name in the title of his first collection, and his mugshot, albeit rendered in hallucinatory hues, on the cover of the first Panther edition (I'm guessing that's him.). *The Worlds of Robert F. Young* (1965) gathers sixteen of the best stories published in his first two decades as a writer, many of them first appearing in **The Magazine of Fantasy and Science Fiction**. Perhaps the best story is 'Romance in a Twenty-First-Century Used-Car Lot', a story that exists at the interface of SF and surrealism. It has what I would call a textbook opening, simultaneously introducing us immediately to the theme of the story and awakening our curiosity: 'The car-dress stood on a pedestal in the Big Jim display window...'

What in the world is a car-dress, the reader wonders? The only way to find out is to read on. It turns out that in the twenty-first century cars have become as indispensable as clothing. One literally feels naked without a car. This is an anti-automobile satire occupying the same territory

The June 1963 issue of Amazing contained the first of a two part serialisation of The Programmed People which would be collected by Ace in 1965 as a single paperback; Ultimatum in 2050 AD. Art by Ed Emshwiller.

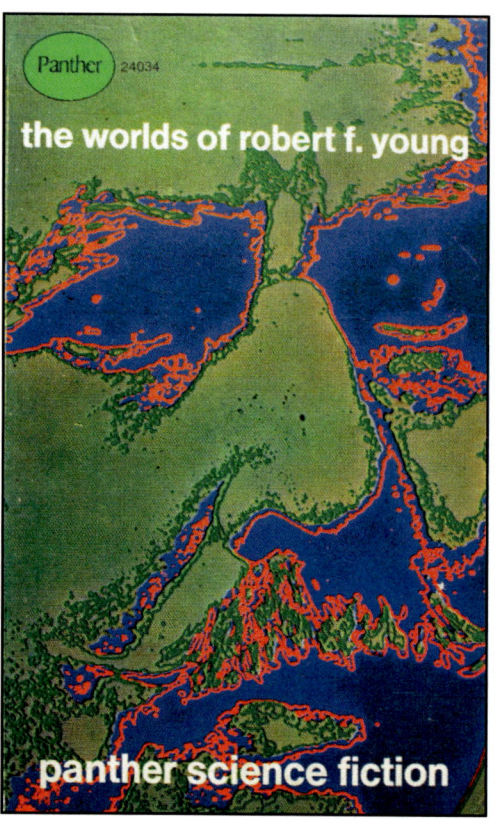

as Ray Bradbury's story 'The Pedestrian' (in which a man is arrested for walking!). Young's use of sentimentality is also reminiscent of Bradbury's – you may or may not approve. For my own part, I find that this quality, in small doses, can be quite effective.

Another tale in the collection, 'Hopsoil', reads on one level almost like a Bradbury spoof. Purporting to be a translation of a Martian SF story, it tells of a visit to the third planet by denizens of the fourth. Amid the ruins of a dead terrestrial civilization the visitors find that Earth's soil, which is famously blue, is capable of growing beer trees from discarded beer bottles, hence the punning title. In its playfulness this story is typical Young.

Another story with a punning title is 'Flying Pan'. The heroine of this tale, a shy young woman who moves from a quiet US village to a bustling metropolis, where she feels out of place, could have stepped straight out of the pages of an O. Henry yarn. Maybe this is the kind of story the great short story pioneer would have written if he had been a fantasy/SF writer.

'Emily and the Bards Sublime' is a short, sweet tale about the curatrix of a museum in which android recreations of celebrated poets declaim their most famous verses to non-existent crowds of visitors. Emily is distraught to learn that her beloved poets must make way for a permanent display of 20th century automobiles (Young again vents his animus against cars!). In the end she devises an effective compromise.

Her eyes were twin pools in which you might drown. How many times have you read that sentence, or one much like it, in a novel or short story? In 'Goddess in Granite' Young takes this hackneyed metaphor and makes it into a literal reality, thereby revitalizing it. He

---

Top - The Worlds of Robert Young was a 1966 collection of 16 of Young's shorts which invariably draw on MoF&SF. Pictured is the 1968 UK paperback edition from Panther.

Bottom - Ed Emsh illustration for Young's 'Romance in a 21st Century Used-Car Lot' for a 1960 issue of MoF&SF.

attempts something similar in his short novel *The Last Yggdrasil* (1982, expanded from a novella in **F & S F** 1959) but the result is much less effective. It is the story of a woodsman hired to chop down a giant tree by the colonists of an alien planet, whose houses, situated in the shade, are starting to rot due to transpiration. The woodsman experiences guilt at the destruction of this arboreal marvel, taking the form of hallucinations – but are they? – of a dryad. At only 135 pages long in the Ballantine edition, this is a short novel but I started to weary of it long before the end. John Buchan wrote a much better tale about a dryad whose home is being destroyed: 'The Grove of Ashtaroth' (1910).

A better novel than *The Last Yggdrasil* is *Eridahn* (1983). A man from the 1990s travels back in time to the Cretaceous period to investigate a strange, anomalous fossil. He meets two kids who, in spite of appearances, are Martians who have been kidnapped and brought to 'Eridahn' – the Martian name for Earth, which translates as 'Zooland', a reference to the array of strange creatures i.e. dinosaurs, that live there. One of the children is literally a Princess of Mars, a clue that Young is writing an ERB homage. The dinosaurs make us think of the Caprona of *The Land that Time Forgot* and its sequels.

Unlike the over-earnest *The Last Yggdrasil*, this novel is great fun, a rip-roaring adventure, a Burroughs tribute with improved writing. The story begins in the thick of the action, thus circumventing the boring preliminary chapters one often gets in novels of this ilk. It is inventive in its details but with no particular aspiration towards originality in its main theme. The book's hero, Carpenter, drives around in a 'triceratank', a 'reptivehicle' that, thanks to an illusion field, resembles a ceratopsian. He is able to communicate with the children thanks to translating devices that fit into the wearer's ears. Not an original idea by any means but I like the name Young gives to them: hearrings.

Martians are humans indeed but at the age of thirteen they undergo a process called desentimentalization, which is supposed to make them more rational à la Mr. Spock but instead has made them cold, ruthless and greedy. Young is criticized in *The Encyclopedia of SF* for being over-sentimental, and I guess this is his rebuke to his critics.

Carpenter takes the children under his wing, protecting them from the vicious kidnappers who fly around in 'pteranodon' planes. He flees to a quarry where he meets an old book-loving hermit, who reminded me of Ballard, the character in *Logan's Run*. Indeed, this character has a writer's name also: Huxley.

Eridahn is an enjoyable book, easily living up to the promise of Darrell Sweet's thrilling cover painting. Young's prose is a pleasure to read – precise, picturesque and often lightly humorous.

Both *The Last Yggdrasil* and *Eridahn* were originally novellas published in mags but later expanded to novel length. The same is true of *The Vizier's Second Daughter* (1985), which was based on 'City of Brass' (**Amazing Stories**, Aug. 1965). Maybe in his relative old age Young found it harder to generate new ideas than to revisit old ones.

I haven't read *The Vizier's Second Daughter* but 'City of Brass' is another very enjoyable work. It proposes a science fictional explanation for some of the marvels that can be found in the tales of the Arabian Nights. This is indeed a favourite method of Young – SF reworkings of much-loved tales. In 'Boarding Party' (**Amazing Stories**, Sept. 1963), his chosen template is Jack and The Beanstalk. Considerably less ingenious than this is 'Rumpelstiltskinski' (**Amazing Stories**, June 1965). Better than either is 'The Thousand Injuries of Mr. Courtney' (**Fantastic**, July 1964), an SF riff on a short story by Honoré De Balzac. Who else but Young would think of such a thing?

By a happy coincidence, the same issue of **Fantastic** that contains this story also contains one of the very best tales by the second member of my triumvirate, Jack Sharkey (1931 – 1992). In 'The Venus Charm', a spaceman named Rogan crash-lands on an extremely bizarre planet that seems to be all desert – monotonous, unbroken to the distant horizon. But the sand on which he walks is not conven-

Michael Herring's painting of an intergalactic lumberjack haunted by doubts for this 1982 Del Rey novel.

Have triceratank, will travel. Darrell K Sweet painting for the 1983 Del Rey edition.

tional sand – the grains are colloidal crystals that gradually turn to a glue-like liquid under the heat of the sun. Rogan realizes he will drown in the stuff in a few hours at most. A dash back to the wrecked spaceship (Rogan's run?) won't save him as this will be engulfed too.

Sharkey brilliantly describes this surrealistic SF landscape, in vocab almost worthy of Clark Ashton Smith. Rogan's only hope, he realizes, lies with the Venus Charm of the title, won during a gambling session with a Venusian. At this point SF melds seamlessly with fantasy. The amulet grants both good fortune and bad, depending on whether it faces outwards on one's chest or inwards. But is Venusian good luck the same as Terran good luck?

Rogan must use all his ingenuity to escape from this predicament.

Wishfulfilment by means of tokens, charms etc. was a favourite theme of Sharkey's. 'Hear and Obey' (**Fantastic**, Sept. 1964) is a light and frothy comedy (at first) in which Aladdin's lamp is purchased from a junk shop by a rather desperate man named Melvin – evidently considered an appropriate 'comedy' name in the US of the 50s and 60s. See, for example, Harvey Kurtzmann's classic cover for **Mad** # 1. But the horrific climax of this story owes less to **Mad** than to E.C. stablemate **Tales From The Crypt**. Artist Schelling provided a serviceable illo but really the job should have gone to Jack Davis!

Title page from Fantastic with a George Schelling illustration for one of Sharkey's 'wish-fulfilment' tales.

1998 anthology whose title was a pun on Harlan Ellison's Dangerous Visions.

Unlike Robert F. Young, Sharkey did not issue any collections of his stories during his lifetime; to find them you must hunt through old mags, or sometimes anthologies. Dangerous Vegetables (1998) contains a lovely little horror comedy called 'No Harm Done' that is well worth seeking out. This Baen compendium was 'created' by Keith Laumer – he was due to edit it but died before he could carry out the task, which instead fell to Martin Greenberg and Charles Waugh.

Sharkey wrote a small number of novels, of which I have read only one. *Ultimatum in 2050 A.D.* (1965) is divided into three parts (a division missing in the original magazine publication as 'The Programmed People, **Amazing Stories**, 1963). Part I, Crisis, describes a future dystopia, a Hive housing ten million inhabitants. The fully automated environment is incapable of supporting more than this number, therefore surplus individuals must be routinely culled, unbeknownst to the population. That we are not meant to take this bleak picture entirely seriously is indicated by Sharkey's choice of name for the hapless hero who joins the rebels fighting the system, plotting to overthrow the state – no, not Melvin but Lloyd Bodger.

The much shorter Part II, Basis, shows us how this dystopia came into being. We are whisked back to 1965, only a couple of years in advance of first publication, so that this story can be seen in part as political satire, an extrapolation of already existing tendencies. Not

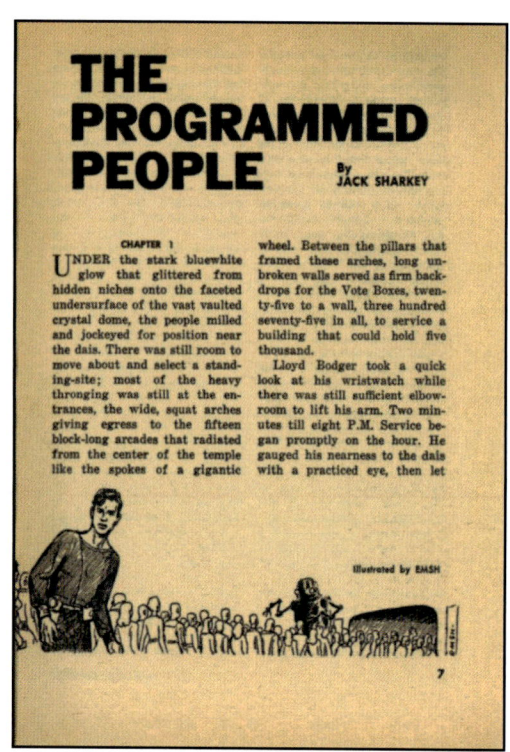

Emsh illustration for the title page for the first part of The Programmed People, from a 1963 issue of Amazing Stories.

surprisingly, this dystopia is really a failed utopia, an attempt to create 'the first real democracy since Ancient Greece'. Advances in electronic communication bring the possibility of direct democracy via voting machines. This opens up comic possibilities (see, for instance, the under-rated British film *The Rise and Rise of Michael Rimmer*, 1969) that Sharkey doesn't exploit to the max, possibly because he was more interested in writing a hybrid comedy/action adventure than an out-and-out farce. Indeed, the novel was published as one half of an Ace Double with some entirely humourless artwork by John Schoenherr, an often brilliant artist but probably the wrong choice for this particular tale. Kelly Freas would have been ideal.

The even shorter Part III, Metamorphosis, is the obligatory happy ending, which seems to me to have been rushed. Bodged, one might say.

The third of my trio is Richard Wilson (1920 – 1987), a member of the Futurians, the writers' group that included such luminaries as Frederik Pohl, Isaac Asimov and Damon Knight.

His first novel, *The Girls From Planet Five* (1955) is set in the future – 1998! – a time when the USA, and indeed much of the globe, is a matriarchy. Great Britain helped to set the trend with a female PM – nice bit of prophecy by Wilson there. The only outpost of masculinity in the US is Texas, to which protagonist Dave Hull, journalist, flees for his sanity, exchanging his car for a 'hoss'. Into this situation alien invaders arrive – the Girls from Planet 5 – another matriarchy but a more extreme one, perhaps a vision of what Earth will become. The girls wear brief silvery uniforms, enabling cover artist Freas to demonstrate his renowned mastery of metallic surfaces, usually confined to spaceships. For good measure there's one of those too, in the top right hand corner; this must be a scout craft, rather than the ship the invaders arrived in, which is one of those vast hovering saucers that always make me think of the 80s mini-series *V*. The girls, or Lyru, are accompanied by spiral-shaped interpreters housed in black boxes; Freas' interpretation of these interpreters is especially imaginative, making them look more like genies of the lamp. All in all, this Lancer paperback, with its purple trimmed pages, is a thing of beauty, well worth seeking out. There is also a Ballantine edition available, with a cover by Richard Powers – nuff said!

Wilson worked in journalism for much of his life, which is reflected in Dave Hull's choice of profession. A news office setting, indeed, is one that he frequently employed in his fiction. It comes as no surprise, for instance, to see that one of the stories in his first collection bears the title 'Press Conference'. This is in fact one of the weaker stories in what is on the whole an impressive gathering. *Those Idiots From Earth,* published by Ballantine in 1957, is hailed on the cover as an original publication not a reprint but in fact most of the contents had already appeared in magazines. The exception is the title story, a deft satire in which machines from outer space attempt to conquer the earth by employing the aid of her most powerful computer. But said computer has divided loyalties!

Wilson has been compared with Fredric Brown (e.g. by David Pringle in *The Ultimate Guide to Science Fiction* 1990, and Allan Bryce in **Infinity** # 10, 2018), a comparison which perhaps overly flatters Wilson although one story in the collection certainly has a strong Brownian flavor. 'Don't Fence Me In' is the shortest story in the book, a little over vignette length. Narrated by an amusing drunk, it tells of how Earth's first attempts at interplanetary

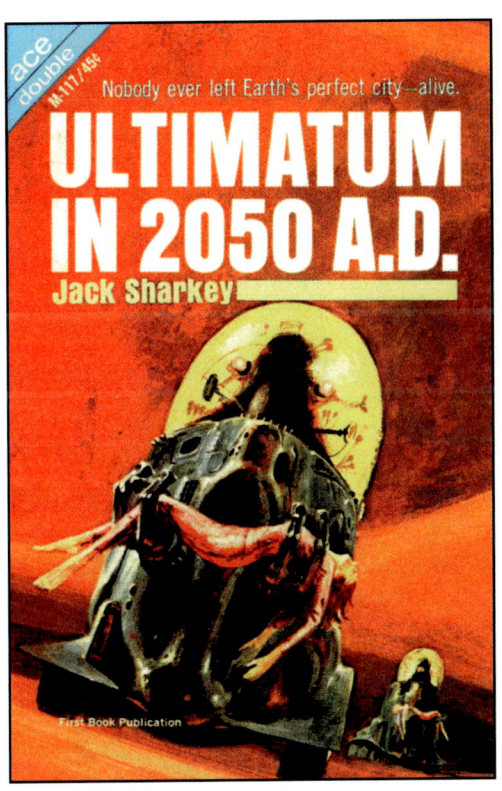

Ace's 1965 repackaging of The Programmed People, which was originally serialised in Amazing. Art by John Schoenherr

1967 edition from Lancer Books with a Kelly Freas cover.

1957 collection of 10 of Wilson's novelettes and shorts, with a Richard Powers cover.

A dozen short stories made up this 1962 collection, also with a Richard Powers cover.

travel were frustrated by the discovery of an invisible barrier around the planet, erected by a Galactic Federation nervous of the human race (and rightly so, one might think!). Without wishing to give too much away, the solution to this problem involves inebriation – certainly a *very* Brownian solution! Shades also of Brown's most famous story 'Arena' (1943), which likewise involves an invisible barrier which must somehow be breached. Despite these influences, 'Don't Fence Me In' stands on its own two feet as a lovely little story, one which encapsulates a very 50s optimism about space travel (an optimism which has sadly evaporated.).

Wilson specialized in humour but he could also do the straight stuff. Examples of the latter in this volume include the novella 'It's Cold Outside', essentially a variant on Huxley's *Brave New World*, and 'Lonely Road', in which a man driving home from work, stopping off at a transport café for a cup of coffee, notices that everyone has vanished. The scenario is anticipatory of the pilot episode of **The Twilight Zone**, 'Where Is Everybody?' – obviously this is a 'puzzle' story, but the solution that Wilson proposes differs from that offered by Rod Serling. 'Lonely Road' has an eeriness worthy of Richard Matheson – the realization that he is alone steals over the protagonist only very gradually – but at the conclusion the disquieting, disturbing atmosphere is leavened, in characteristic Wilson fashion, by something more humane and touching. A skillful story this, playing, like George R. Stewart's *Earth Abides*, on the fear – or is it the fantasy? – of having the world all to oneself. Like much of Wilson's fiction, it is not necessarily staggeringly original but it is well-crafted and sensitively written, the kind of story you can read more than once, savouring the nuances.

Some of the themes explored in Wilson's first collection are revisited in his second, *Time Out For Tomorrow* (1962). 'Kin' has a certain, er, kinship, with 'Those Idiots From Earth', while 'Wasp' ultimately parallels 'Lonely Road', although superficially they are quite dissimilar. 'The Big Fix' begins as a gritty, grimy, slice-of-life depiction of life among some city-dwelling junkies but then shoots off quite unexpectedly into outer space, thanks to a new drug called Uru. I wonder if Stan Lee ever read this story? If memory serves me right, Uru was the name he gave to the metal from which The Mighty Thor's hammer was fashioned.

One of the stories in the collection is cheekily entitled 'The Tunnel Under The World' – the title Wilson's fellow Futurian Frederik Pohl had already used for one of his most famous yarns (filmed in the 60s for BBC TV's *Out of The Unknown*). I was not at all surprised to see on the acknowledgements page that Wilson's story appeared under a different title for its magazine publication.

'An Abundance of Good Things' concerns an invasion by stealth mounted by android aliens – the stuff of nightmares in much SF, such as *Invasion of The Body Snatchers* and Doctor Who's Auton serials, but here treated in a characteristically light and frivolous manner. Comical invasions were indeed a recurring theme in Wilson's fiction; all three of his novels used this concept. In *30 Day Wonder* (1960), the twist is that the aliens are terribly law-abiding, insisting that all Earth laws should be enforced to the letter. I have this novel in the Icon edition of 1963 – the cover artwork is rudimentary, or rudi-awful, but as I have no other Icon paperbacks I'm rather fond of this one.

Wilson published a few other collections in pamphlet form near the end of his life but many of his stories remain uncollected.

Conclusion: It would be quite possible to write a very decent, thorough history of SF that avoided any mention of Messrs. Young, Sharkey or Wilson. Indeed, Brian Aldiss' *Billion Year Spree* is an example of just such a book. They belong on no one's list of the 'bards sublime'. Yet at their best all three produced work that is sparkling, ingenious and, yes, memorable – stories that would enliven any anthology in which they appeared. If there's any justice in the world they will be numbered among 'The Remembered Ones'.

S M GUARIENTO chats to The Paperback Fanatic about his new book - Light into Ink- A Critical Survey of 50 Film Novelisations.

TRIPPING THE INK FANTASTIC

Congratulations on the very impressive *Light Into Ink*, a book that I think will interest many readers of The Paperback Fanatic. Maybe you could tell everyone a bit more about it.
Thanks Justin. *Light into Ink* is an in-depth study of the film novelization, or movie tie-in, approached through 50 representative case studies. These are collected into eight "themed" sections – so, for example, there are chapters on Antichrist movies, Italian cult films, End-of-the-World epics and Visionary Cinema. The latter is a conveniently broad umbrella heading, covering everything from *X – The Man With the X-Ray Eyes* to *Performance*. There are also sections devoted to the work of filmmakers John Carpenter and David Cronenberg, whose early films enjoyed a lengthy run of tie-ins. The chief focus is on SF, horror and fantasy titles, mainly because the speculative genres – in my experience – seem to lend themselves more readily to creative expansion in prose. But the book also covers comedies, westerns, thrillers and midnight movies. The idea was to cover a broad enough spectrum of titles to illustrate my main thesis, which is that novelizations work best as "alternative histories" of the film narrative – reinventing their source in sometimes startling new ways, with new story material, new characters, even radical new subtexts.

Can you explain what you mean by "alternative histories" in this context?
Sure. In science-fiction terms, an alternative history (or "counter-factual") takes historical events that we know happened one way, and presents them in quite another – setting up a rival reality inside our imaginations, which contradicts our memories of the factual events themselves. (The most oft-used example being, "What if the Nazis won WW2?") The cognitive dissonance effect this generates, as the mind tries to reconcile the two contradictory realities, can be extremely interesting. Novelizations work in a similar way. The creative process of adapting a film script into

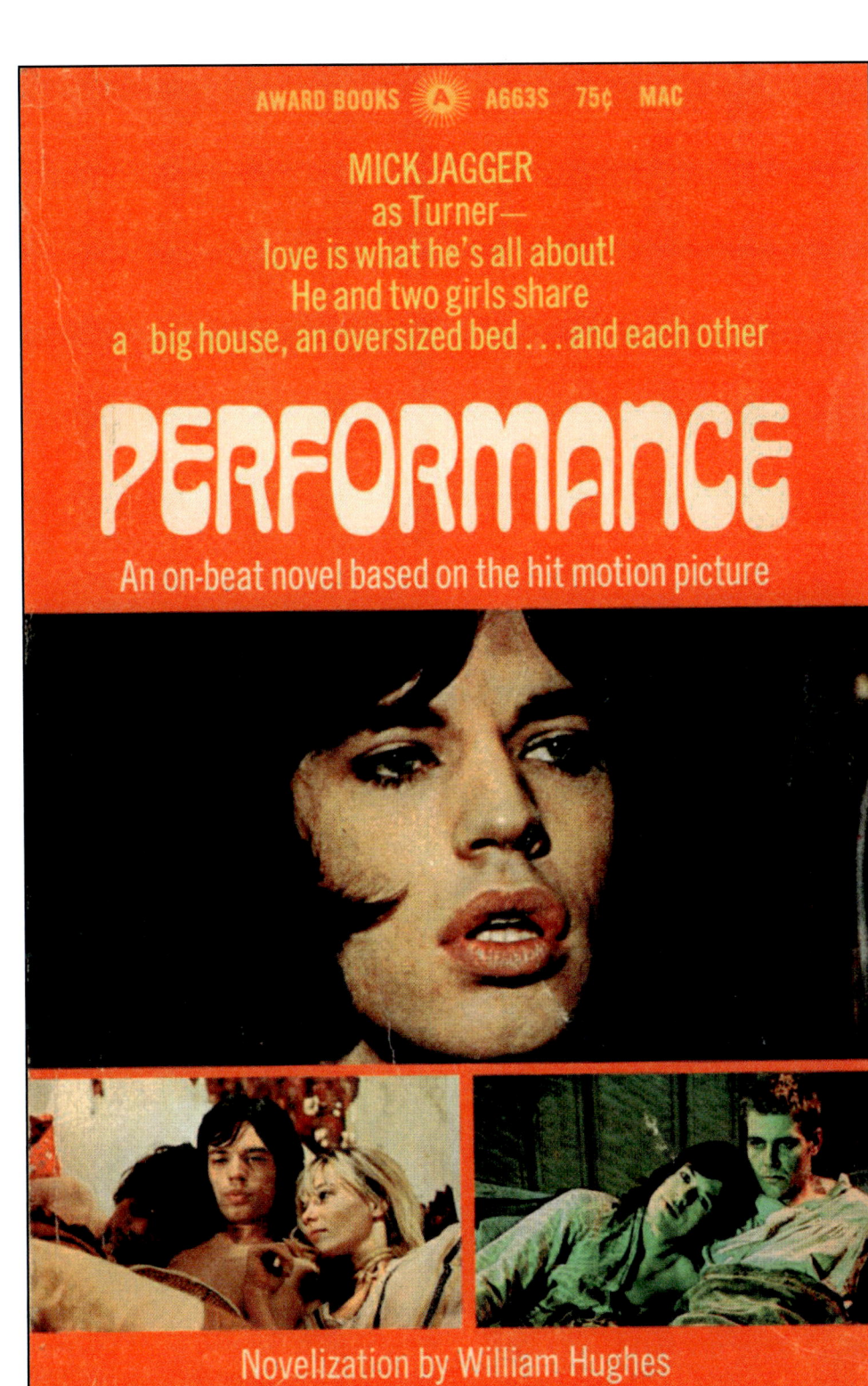

prose involves all kinds of adjustments to the source, minor and major, in order to translate the narrative into the new medium. Prose equivalents must be found for cinematic ideas. Characterisations must be explored in more depth. The question of narrative voice must be addressed – whose perspective is the story to be told from? Would a third-, or first-person narrative work best? The net result of these myriad changes – plus the inclusion of scenes (and sometimes characters) deleted from the final cut of the film itself – is to subtly alter the focus and tenor of the narrative, so that the reader experiences the story in quite a different way to the filmgoer. Each can enhance the other in quite interesting ways.

MTIs often include extra scenes which never made it into the film's "final cut". The original King Kong novelization [by Delos W. Lovelace] famously includes the deleted "spider pit" sequence in full, for instance. But are there examples of tie-ins which diverge more substantially from the films they're based on? Most novelizations differ only slightly from the film, as studios often insist that the novelizer sticks faithfully to the source. But a creative author can reinvent (and even sometimes subvert) the film in radical new ways. Take Michael Robson's novelization of Holocaust 2000, for example (Sphere 1978). While the film is a straight knock-off of The Omen, with Simon Ward's Anti-Christ clearly satanic in origin, the novel offers an alternative, secular reading in direct opposition to the film. The explicitly supernatural events of the film are presented here in a far more ambiguous light, causing us to re-evaluate all the characters and their motivations. Fascinating stuff. In a similar vein is the late Dennis Etchison's tie-in for Halloween III – Season of the Witch (US: Jove 1982/UK: Star 1983), published under his "Jack Martin" alias. The film, again, is a straight horror yarn in the style of Invasion of the Body Snatchers, with a gruff hero battling a Celtic demon and his android bogey-men. And great fun it is too. But Etchison cleverly pitches the story as the paranoid delusion of our schizoid

Sphere's first tie-in edition to Holocaust 2000 from 1978, one of genre of devil-kid films in the wake of The Omen.

hero, while also incorporating deleted story material from writer Nigel Kneale's original script draft. The book turns an essentially lightweight horror piece into something much darker, deeper and more sophisticated.

Movie tie-ins have enjoyed an enduring popularity with readers and collectors, what would you attribute this to?
That's a tricky question. Collectors often hoard them simply as souvenirs, maybe more for their jacket art than their content (which, admittedly, is rarely top-notch). And once upon a time, in the days before home video, tie-ins served as handy *aides-memoires*, allowing us to relive our favourite films (and TV shows) in between their usually-infrequent television screenings. But the popularity of

novelizations long predates cinema. Theatrical novelizations have existed since the Shakespearian era, and continue to sell. Modern iterations include novelizations of computer games, musicals, even rock albums. Some writers have even novelized novelizations, taking the concept to delirious extremes. Turning things into books seems to be an obsession of the print era. I can't really offer any profound explanation for this, other than that we love to read, to create pictures in our minds. Movie tie-ins invite us to recreate films in the "projection booth" of the imagination, running them alongside our memories of the films themselves. Bringing us back, again, to alternative histories.

What set you off on the road to collecting MTIs?
That's an easy one! The *Doctor Who* range, from Target Books. I started watching the show during the latter part of the Jon Pertwee era – so probably 1973, making me about six years old. Something about the idea of transformation seems to have intrigued me from an early age. Bodily changes. Men turning into Things. All very Freudian. Transformation formed a good part of *Doctor Who*'s weekly storylines – and the fact that the hero *himself* could transform, changing before my eyes from Pertwee to Tom Baker, only cemented the show's appeal. And then I found that the series itself had transformed, from television images into prose, via Target's wonderful tie-in range. Dozens of pocket-sized paperbacks, all with dazzling jacket art – most, at that time, by the Cypriot artist Chris Achilleos. I was hooked from the start. The idea that a TV show, or a film, could be captured inside a book fascinated me. So much so that a few years later, aged eleven, I even tried my hand at writing novelizations myself: *Doctor Who, Flash Gordon's Trip to Mars, Frankenstein and the Monster from Hell*... All with hand-drawn jacket art and glossy Sticky Back Plastic covers, naturally. Every one a priceless collector's item.

At eleven years old, how did you go about adapting these films and TV shows? Presumably you didn't have access to the original scripts?
No, absolutely not. My first novelizations were more impressive as feats of memory than as prose. Working from notes hastily jotted during TV broadcasts, my earliest adaptations were broad-brush recollections of key events and dialogue earnestly transcribed into school notebooks. Christmas 1979 introduced a technological revolution: the portable audio-cassette recorder. Films and television episodes could now be taped in full, enabling me to transcribe dialogue and events with total accuracy. But transcription proved to be a tedious slog, and after a couple of dogged tape-to-novel experiments (*Blake's 7* and *King of the Rocket Men*), my enthusiasm waned. It

KKLAK! The iconic Chris Achilleos illustration for Doctor Who and the Dinosaur Invasion from 1976.

was finally killed off completely by the home video revolution. The need to preserve my favourite films and shows on paper seemed suddenly less urgent now that the originals were readily available on tape. My career as a novelizer ended overnight.

But you retained an interest in novelizations, clearly.
Yes, a trace fascination for the concept stuck with me. Turning film into prose, light into ink – something about it just appeals to me. That obsession for transformation again. Over the next 40 years or so, the focus of my interest gradually sharpened. Writing the Book of the Film was no longer an ambition. But what about the Book of the Books of the Film...? And so the idea for *Light into Ink* clicked into place.

There are so many MTIs, how did you go about whittling down to the 50 books you reviewed?
I think they call it an organic process, a technical term for trial and error. I knew roughly the books I wanted to cover – the Carpenter/Cronenberg titles were a must, as were the Dollars Trilogy, the *Mad Max* novels, and so on. I also knew I wanted to include a few foreign-language titles, to address the "international experience" of the tie-in – something I hadn't really seen covered elsewhere, beyond the French-language works of academic Jan Baetens (currently the go-to guy on transmedialization studies). The final roster fell into place by a process of elimination, essentially. The films and the books adapted from them had to be interesting enough to sustain the kind of forensic analysis I had in mind. They also had to fit broadly into the eight umbrella categories I settled on for the book. As *Light*

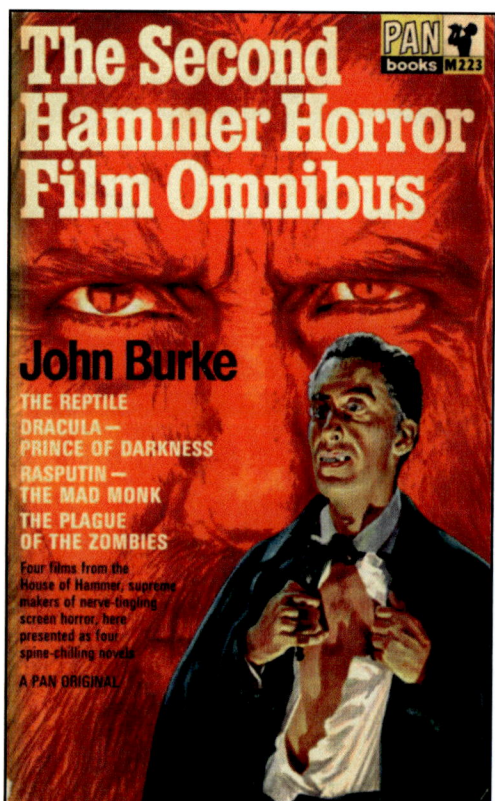

into Ink took shape, a number of proposed chapters fell by the wayside: a section devoted to John Burke, one to Hammer Horrors (with nods to Amicus, Tyburn et al)... Those ended up being whittled down to a single chapter on *Moon Zero Two*, which offered the "alternative history" angle I was looking for.

How does the final book compare to the one you started on day one?
It's actually surprisingly close. I knew I wanted each chapter to serve as a kind of "condensed version" of the novel, giving the reader a sense of its best (and worst) qualities, and illustrating my points with sizeable extracts from the books. And of course a strong visual layout was important from the start. With the kind of dense forensic examination I proposed, it was vital to break up the text with as many illustrations as I could find. Hopefully I've achieved that!

Were there any books that you wanted to review but couldn't track down? For instance, the original editions of the H G Lewis tie-ins to his splatter movies are impossible to find.
Ah, the ones that got away... Actually, there's only one I can think of: the tie-in for Dan Coscarelli's *Phantasm*, written by the director's mother (Kate Coscarelli, now a writer of romantic fiction). The novelization was originally issued as a Japanese exclusive, but was later published in English in a limited run of 500 copies. Really hard to get hold of. But in the end, it wouldn't have fit into the structure of the book I'd chosen, so I don't really regret its exclusion. The Japanese tie-in market is something I'd like to see covered in more depth, as there have been some interesting exclusives published there (including one for Ridley Scott's *Prometheus*, by Joe Spies and Damon Lindelhof). Any Japanophile Fanatic readers up for the job?

I think there is a bit of a story to you being able to cover the MTI to Suspiria?
Ha, you could say that... The novelization of *Suspiria* was an Italian exclusive by Neo-Noir author Nicola Lombardi, first issued as part of a Dario Argento anthology called *Terrore Profondo* (Newton & Compton 1997) – not unlike the old *Hammer Horror Film Omnibus* volumes published by Pan in the Sixties. In addition to translating Lombardi's novella (which runs to around 90 pages in length), I also decided to go back and translate the original 277-page screenplay by Argento and Daria Nicolodi, to compare and contrast all three versions of the tale: the script, the film and the tie-in. Madness! That chapter alone took around six months to complete, as I had not only to translate Italian into English, but into *readable* English – and also wrap my head around Italian screenplay notation, which differs in many respects from the Anglo-American format (and includes initially-puzzling technical references to MDP, PPP, FC and so on...these being, respectively, *the camera* [macchina da presa], *extreme close-up* [primissimo piano] and *offscreen* [fuori campo]). To complicate my life still further, I decided to translate the relevant portions from Argento's autobiography *Paura* as well, and include sections from that alongside the script and novella extracts... Nineteen nervous breakdowns later, the finished chapter offers a fair bit to interest Argento devotees – including scenes from the script that were never filmed, like a heavily-stylised prologue and a languidly erotic reverie referencing Maxfield Parrish. So my sanity was not sacrificed in vain.

I have always held a doubt about the worth of MTIs as a read. What are the MTIs that you would give me to read to change my mind?
You should certainly check out the titles I cover in Part 8, which is specifically devoted to the best examples of the form. *Forbidden Planet* by "W.J. Stuart" [Philip MacDonald] is a smart epistolary reconstruction of the film (with darker hints to the underlying sexual subtext);

Light Into Ink finishes on a chapter titled 'Ne plus ultra: or, That's How It Done' which highlights some of Guariento's favourite tie-ins. Including Monte Carlo or Bust!

Nigel Kneale's novelization of his own *Quatermass* (Arrow 1979) supplies a wealth of additional material, and some heart-rendingly poignant character detail; and Anne Carlisle's quirky adaptation of cult favourite *Liquid Sky* (Doubleday/Dolphin 1987), the 1983 film she co-wrote and starred in, turns novelization into a fascinating branch of autobiography. Best of the lot, however, are Richard Elman's *Taxi Driver* (US: Bantam/UK: Corgi 1976) and E.W. Hildick's *Monte Carlo or Bust* (UK: Sphere/US: Berkley Medallion 1969, a.k.a. *Those Daring Young Men in Their Jaunty Jalopies*). *Taxi Driver* is a frankly superb piece of vernacular poetry, a vital companion-piece to the film told in the voice of its psychotic anti-hero. And *Monte Carlo or Bust* takes a slightly unpromising concept – the novelization of a slapstick comedy sequel to *Those Magnificent Men in Their Flying Machines* – and transforms it into a flat-out hilarious avant-garde masterpiece. Mixing prose, script excerpts and typographical jokes, the novel even mimics certain cinematic devices (split-screen effects, fadeouts and so on). And the footnotes are sublime. Without a doubt, *Monte Carlo* is the most purely enjoyable title I cover in the book – and could be the most enjoyable novelization of all time. I first read it when I was around 9 or 10 years old, and it stuck with me for the next 30-odd years. So much so that I later found, to my horror, that I'd inadvertently ripped-off one of its typographical gags in my novel *Incarnadine*. Is it too late to call it an homage...?

Any other MTIs that stand out for being particularly memorable, for good or bad reasons?

Honourable mentions should go to Robson's *Holocaust 2000* and Etchison's *Halloween III*, which we touched on earlier. Another Robson title that's a must-read is *Hardcore* (Sphere 1977), his adaptation of the Fiona Richmond porn movie (issued under his "Philip Massinger" pseudonym). An amazingly erudite and witty novel, by a part-time Shakespearian scholar and smut-peddler. There's Phil Smith's *Incredible Melting Man*, of course (NEL 1978), a lurid slice of pulp horror which expands considerably on its source with some fascinating, even moving nods to the work of

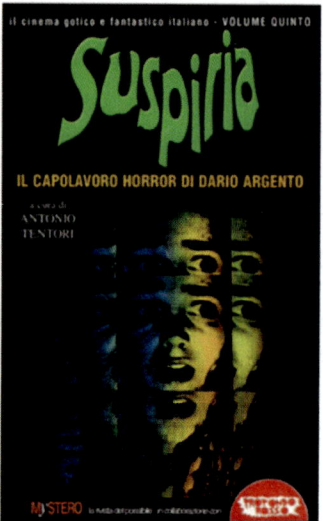

Above - sample spreads from Light Into Ink, which is available through Amazon in both a deluxe colour edition and a midnight back-and-white edition.

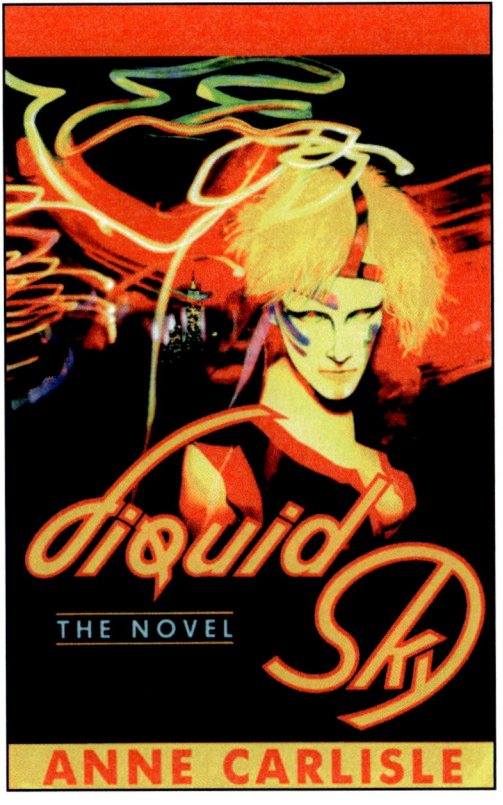
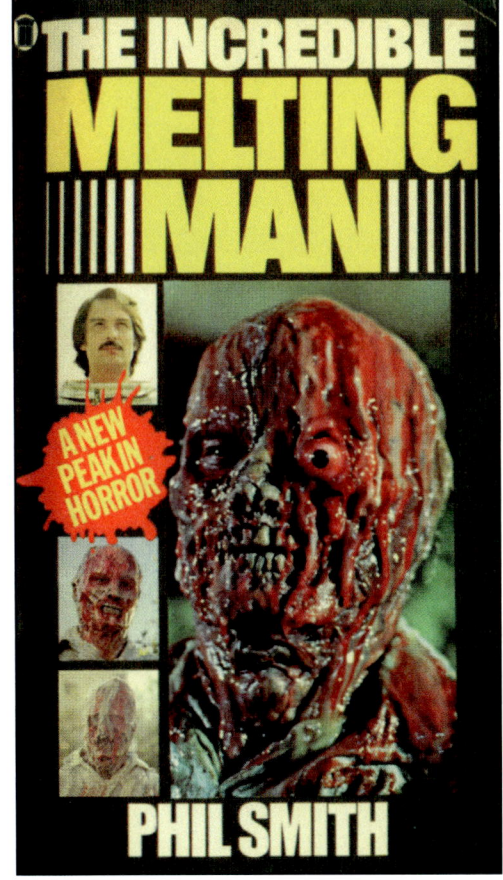

Nigel Kneale. And Mike McQuay's *Escape from New York* (US: Bantam/UK: Corgi 1981) is a terrific read, bolstering the Carpenter film with some hard-edged realism and meaty backstories for its leads. Alan Dean Foster's *Dark Star* (US: Ballantine 1974/UK: Futura 1979) is also worth your time, offering a mournful take on Carpenter's antic debut; the ending, in particular, is touchingly conceived and executed. Even better is the novelization of Peter Weir's *The Last Wave*, by Romanian expat Petru Popescu (Australia: Angus & Robertson/UK: Arrow 1978), a beautifully stylish and poetic novel which supplies the transcendent ending Weir considers missing from his cut. As for the memorably bad... Well, *Scanners II – The New Order* by "Professor Janus Kimball" [i.e. Richard Hack – and yes, that *is* his real name] must hold some record for wilful misuse of the English language. I suspect the author was taking the piss – that pen-name certainly suggests so – though in this game, it's not always easy to tell.

What project will you work on next?
Too soon to say. *Light into Ink* came about purely by accident, simply as a means of killing time before I found a subject for my second novel. The pieces were originally planned to be posted on my website, and conceived on a much smaller scale. Bit by bit, they began to grow into something far larger than I'd imagined. And by then it was too late…
Maybe I'll go back and give those juvenile novelizations of mine a polish. You have been warned!

Thanks for your time. You've certainly made me reconsider my views on MTIs. And best of luck with that King of the Rocketmen novelisation!

RICHARD PÉREZ SEVES chats to The Paperback Fanatic about his mission to bring the art and careers of fetish artists such as Eric Stanton and Gene Bilbrew back into the public's eye.

UNMASKING STANTON

I think most readers of this zine will know who Eric Stanton is, but would you mind recapping and perhaps more importantly explain why you think his fetish art is important and has endured?
What's important to remember about Eric Stanton is that he was not only a pioneer of fetish art, but the first "career" fetish artist—meaning that early on he made a decision to dedicate his life to the making of fetish art. It was a choice, not something he fell into by accident or did for a while to earn money, unlike Joe Shuster or the post-porn era incarnation of Bill Ward. Prior to Stanton there were other fetish artists, like Carlo in France, and John Willie, who was British. Carlo produced fetish art for a decade or so; John Willie viewed fetish art as a "hobby," declined commissions, despised merchants like Irving Klaw, etc. Although Stanton was influenced by both of these artists, his intention was always to make a living as a fetish artist. To follow his muse, but also sustain himself financially through fetish art so he could continue doing it. This required a different, more practical mind-set; it necessitated getting inside other people's heads, developing empathy to illustrate other people's dreams and fantasies. For this reason, Stanton hooked up with Irving Klaw, who he took on as a role model and accepted commissions throughout his life. "Eneg" (a.k.a. Gene Bilbrew), who Stanton "discovered" in 1951, was the first of many artists who essentially followed in Stanton's footsteps. So why has Stanton's art endured? For one thing, as Steve Ditko acknowledged, Stanton had a knack for drawing beautiful women. But more than that, Stanton had the unique ability to empathize with outcasts and convey psychological truth. This truth was often conveyed in facial expressions or the body language of his characters, particularly his women—often you don't need dialogue to understand what's going on: the subtext is evident. Stanton also deeply understood male shame—in addition to shame-conditioned

Richard Pérez Seves, author of the brilliant 2018 book Stanton and the History of the Bizarre Underground.

masculine terrors. In fact, Stanton's specialty was in exploiting masculine terrors. In the scenarios he's probably best known for, Stanton's women inevitably came out on top by exposing male weakness. The fact that his women looked beautiful while gaining the upper hand, made it all the more humiliating and unsettling. There's a lot of black comedy in Stanton's work, like the kind you see in Roman Polanski's *Bitter Moon*. You also see a lot of this humour in Stanton's 1960s paperback covers.

How did you develop an interest in fetish art?
I've always had a strong interest in misfits and outcasts—subcultures not embraced or supported by the mainstream. Years ago, in the pre-Internet days, this led me to hang out a lot in Manhattan's East Village where I was exposed to a lot of marginal subcultures and I collected all sorts of marginal artefacts too. I fell in love with Something Weird Video and all sorts of cult and foreign films and comix and fanzines. But it wasn't until I started trading on eBay, likely looking for exploitation-film related stuff, that I really started seeing vintage fetish art. I just thought it was interesting: dark and subversive and of course sexy. What's not to like? You might say my curiosity led me there, and I started purchasing old stuff and began to distinguish between artists like John Willie and Eric Stanton. Then there was the history of this stuff, which I found fascinating. I mean, the world of underground publishers surrounding Stanton in the 1950s and '60s was full of constant drama. Law enforcement authorities, self-righteous postal inspectors, and the FBI were always trying to shut them down. Back then fetish art was lumped together with gay and trans culture—and it was all "deviant" and considered morally wrong—even "anti-American." So making fetish art was an act of rebellion against the status quo. Stanton and Bilbrew were essentially borderline outlaws. Even now, Stanton and Bilbrew still catch all sorts of heat

Displays of sleaze paperbacks with Eric Stanton covers from the Los Angeles art show curated by Richard in 2015.

from mainstream comic fans who see the material as corrupt. Facebook and Instagram habitually shadow-ban or remove non-pornographic fetish art images under the pretense that it's not "family friendly." The problem is that it's not corporate friendly, which is exactly why it's important. It angers me that generations of Americans are allowing to have their tastes shaped by corporate culture—and no one is rebelling against this.

You once co-curated a Stanton art show in LA?
Via eBay, I'd sold some stuff to Dian Hanson, Taschen's sexy-book editor, who informed me that Benedikt Taschen was putting together a show. Anyway, she kept asking me questions about Stanton and people like Irving Klaw, and she soon realized that my knowledge of this stuff went deep—that I was one of these subculture-obsessed weirdos with tunnel vision, ha-ha; and finally the decision was made to put me on salary for two weeks at a thousand a week, fly me out to LA, put me up in a hotel to help them with the show. I was co-curator and essentially the archivist and all-around vintage fetish art nerd. By then, I was already planning a visual history of Eric Stanton—something that went far beyond what they had done—so my research into fetish art and Eric Stanton was fresh and extensive; I had binders and binders of notes and art samples. My job was to lend some historical accuracy to the show and help them identify the art. It was my one and only visit to Los Angeles, which I liked a lot.

How did the deal with Schiffer to publish the Stanton book come about?
I'd pitched my book to numerous publishers, and they were simply the ones who responded

to it first. In other words, it was a matter of putting together a detailed book proposal and showing it to them. I went one step further in showing them a chapter by chapter layout of the entire book on PDF. The book took a long time to come out, much to my chagrin. Well over two years. In the meantime, I self-published a book on Charles Guyette, who was the predecessor of Irving Klaw and the first person to sell fetish art in America. Dita Von Teese championed the book on social media, which really helped me out. Personally, I really love the Guyette book. Self-publishing can sometimes be a pleasure. With traditional publishing everything takes very long and the process is dragged out for years and years.

The level of research in the book is amazing –please tell us about the process of writing it?
I'm obsessive when it comes to research. Underground comic art, in particular, is not taken seriously—fetish art even less so—so I really wanted to dig in, provide citations for all my research—in short, create a serious history, not just a book filled with cut-and-paste rumours like you often see on the Internet. The real difficulty for me was in weaving in the stories of the people surrounding Stanton—the publishers—while making sure it was still a book about Stanton. In other words, I didn't want the book to be like a collection of articles; I wanted a linear narrative largely told from Stanton's point of view. I wanted to make sure that Stanton was the star of the show—the "A" story—while all the rest remained the "B" story. So I would go into the history of Irving Klaw and other underground publishers, but always finding a way to bring it back to Stanton. All the publishers in the book—Irving Klaw, Edward Mishkin, Leonard Burtman, and Stanley Malkin—deserve their own book so it was hard not letting these other characters "take over" or upstage Stanton. But that was the challenge.

There are many, many very rare illustrations in the book. How did you source them?
Some are from the Stanton family but many are from my own Stanton collection, stuff that I've accumulated over the years. When I started trading on eBay, I soon became obsessive about getting Stanton material, in particular. I used other online sites as well, like AbeBooks.com, etc. I've purchased Stanton booklets and art from around the world, including Russia and Japan.

You cover the Stanton contributions to the Satellite paperbacks with their imprints After Hours, First Niter etc. I think these are an outstanding body of art that creates its own universe. What is your take on these books?

In many ways, Stanton's paperback art from the '60s is his most accessible work. The bright colors and gentle humor make them fun. The tone of Stanton's art is very different than the work he did for Irving Klaw and others. There's actually very little darkness in the paperback artwork, and this might reflect Stanton's mood at the time. Stanley Malkin, who was behind the paperback imprints, had put Stanton on salary, even including an all-expenses paid apartment in Manhattan. Basically, this was the most stable, care-free period in Eric Stanton's life. He still shared a studio with Steve Ditko, which meant he had creative company during the day, and at night he had a nice apartment to come home to. One thing I should mention: Stanley Malkin's Satellite Publishing Co. imprint was separate from his paperback imprints. In other words, Malkin was a book packager working on behalf of the mob, who first established Satellite Publishing Co. in 1961 as a means of publishing digest-sized magazines (like the magazine **Bound**). That imprint didn't do well under his control and was handed over to a different book packager (Pasquale Giordano, a.k.a. Pat Martin), and then in 1963 Malkin established his interchangeable paperback imprints: First Niter, After Hours, Unique Books, Wee Hours. I once believed that "Satellite" was an umbrella company name that covered all of Malkin's publishing enterprises, but that's wrong: Satellite and the paperback imprints are separate entities. As I detail in the Stanton book, Malkin had success for a while until things fell apart as a result of a police raid on his Queens warehouse. Police raids affected Irving Klaw, Edward Mishkin, Leonard Burtman and, yes, Stanley Malkin. The police were like Storm-troopers then, forever trying to crush the rebellion. Luckily, these publishers had outstanding legal representation. Famed First Amendment attorney Herald Price Fahringer, who later defended Larry Flynt and Al Goldstein, got his start with Malkin, in fact.

I was fascinated by the links between famous comics artist Steve Ditko and Stanton.

Along with collecting Stanton art, I collect vintage Ditko art. And I became expert at identifying Ditko's hand. Most people assume

Photo of Eric Stanton taken by Steve 'Spider-Man' Ditko. Notice the similarity to the castaway snuggling a leather boot in Stanton's cover painting for Paradise Isle.

that Ditko just did a little inking for Stanton, but the truth is that Ditko assumed other aliases. As I point out in the Stanton book, one of those aliases was "Omar." So early on there's a serial with Stanton and Omar splitting/sharing the artwork, and this sort of set the precedent. It's likely that Ditko was on the fence about becoming a full-blown fetish artist. He was obviously interested in the sub-genre because he did so much of it. And again not just inking but contributing original fetish artwork. Stanton and Ditko's collaborative relationship started in 1953 and continued until at least 1978. That's a long time. In the book, I go into Stanton's influence during the creation of Spider-Man. It's a bit complicated, but I recently received a letter from a friend of Steve Ditko who recalled visiting Ditko in 1962 and seeing "Spider-Man art pages on Eric's drawing table and a page from Sweeter Gwen on Steve's." Even more pronounced, I think, is Stanton's influence on Doctor Strange. Anyone who's interested in this sort of thing might want to read chapters 20 and 26 of the hardcover Stanton book. There's no question that Stanton and Ditko were more like brothers than friends. So close that at one point they even shared a single name: "Jon Bee." Years ago, I also corresponded with Steve Ditko. The most amazing letter I received from Steve detailed the police raid on the studio they shared. It blew my mind to see this. This letter deserves a place in a museum. In a separate note, Ditko also recalled Gene Bilbrew.

You've also self-published a heavily-illustrated book about Gene Bilbrew, whom I

Above- the secret origin of Spider-Man? Fetish art from Stanton depicting spider iconography.

imagine is even less a commercial proposition than a book on Stanton. Again, would you tell readers a bit about Bilbrew and his significance?

Gene Bilbrew was the first black career fetish artist in history, nothing less. And he was a true legend. In the book, I refer to Bilbrew and Stanton as the Lennon and McCartney of fetish art. And this is really true. The two artists loved and hated each other, but ultimately defined fetish art in the 1950s and '60s—and for generations to come. One of the reasons I put the book together was to challenge all the rumours of Bilbrew we see on the Internet, another was simply to showcase his talent—he was capable of creating fetish art of great beauty and elegance. Elegance is not something usually associated with Bilbrew, for those familiar with his later paperback covers. For the book, I cherry-picked the best of the best—his rarely-seen 1950s art. I also trace his career as a vocal group singer and a founding member of the Basin Street Boys. And I

 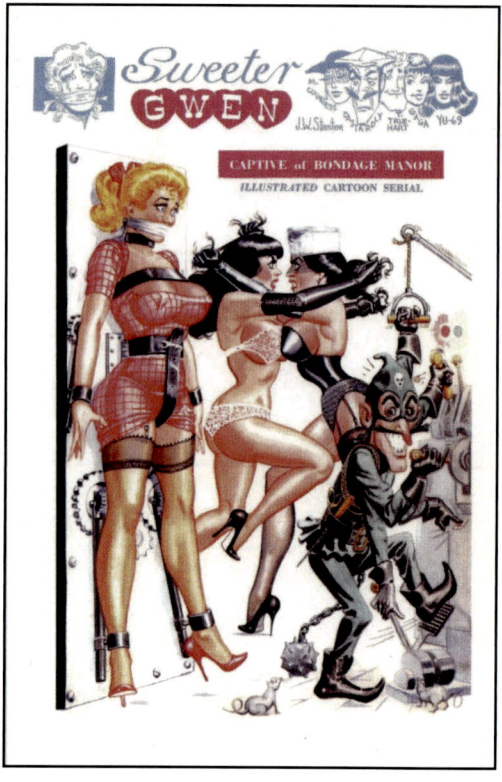

Above - Richard's competitively priced compendiums of rare vintage fetish strips.
Opposite - a selection of Gene Bilbrew's paperback covers. Including a Stanton portrait in Lady Peeper. Also one on the back page middle row in Perpetual Motion. Possibly even Bilbrew in the background.

discovered how he eventually ended up on the East Coast, who his wife was, that he lived in Brooklyn. It was like Bilbrew had lived two uniquely separate lives. By the way, it was the filmmaker Nicolas Winding Refn (the director behind *Drive*, *Pusher*, *Bronson*), who commissioned the research on Bilbrew. So I'm grateful to him for that.

You have also been restoring old fetish strips and publishing them in very affordable editions. What can you tell us about this programme of reprints?

So far, because I've had access to original Stanton art, I've put out two books: *The Return of Gwendoline & Other Bizarre Art* and *Sweeter Gwen*. One of the reasons that so few people know about fetish art is because most of the stuff is out of print. Real vintage copies are priced insanely high. So I thought: what if I reconstruct the booklets but make them even better than the original publications? So that's what I did. I'm really pleased with the quality of both. I'm hoping by pricing the books so low that a new audience will discover this sub-genre of art and not be afraid of it. Even regular comic book fans. I mean, there's nothing to fear. Fetish art, as Steve Ditko understood, is simply outsider art; it's art that pushed the envelope. It can be appreciated by anyone. A big thanks to those who have supported my Eric Stanton, Gene Bilbrew, and Charles Guyette projects. In a strange way, the books are all interlinked.

Thanks for taking the time out to talk to us Richard, and for all of the work you are doing in researching and documenting this often neglected area of popular culture.

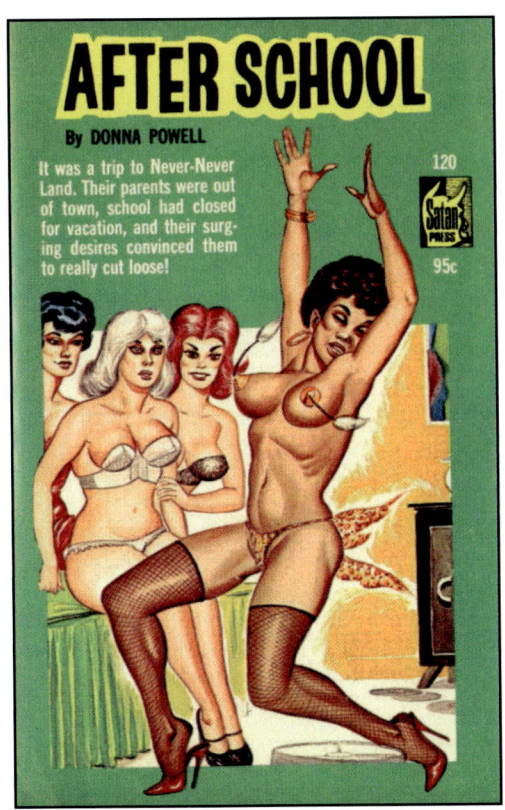
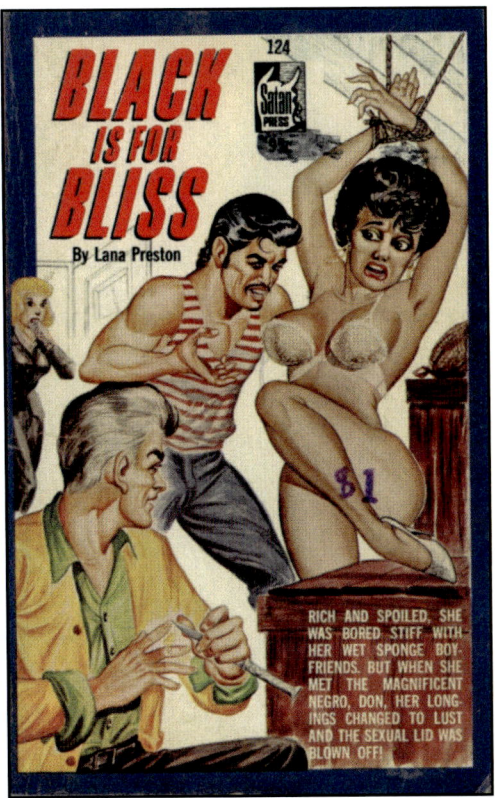
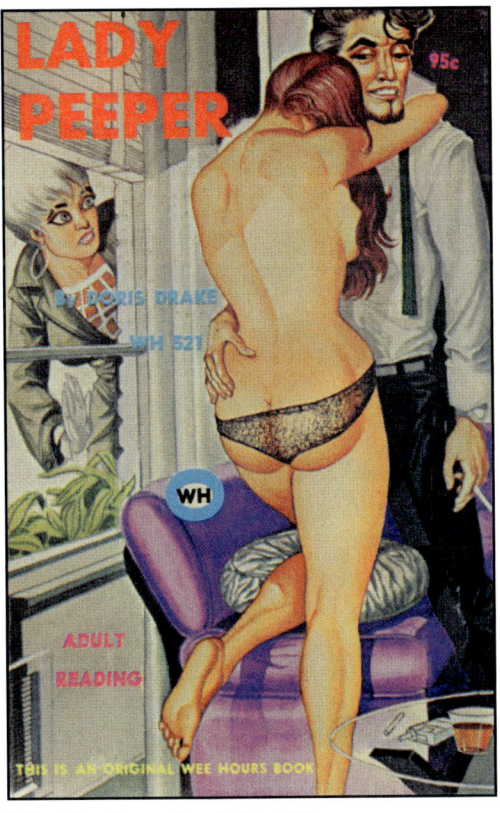

BILL CUNNINGHAM of Pulp 2.0 Press talks about his love of pulp culture in all media and his mission to bring classic material to a modern audience.

MAD PULP BASTARD

Bill, you're the owner of Pulp 2.0 Press and once described as a "mad pulp bastard"! Maybe you could start by sharing your personal journey to becoming a mad pulp bastard....

I was born in 1963 in Oak Park, Illinois, a suburb of Chicago. My family moved around the midwest until my parents became tired of the snow and we moved to the sleepy town of Aiken, South Carolina. The week we moved to Aiken was the 1st time in over a decade that it snowed in SC.

Aiken is a town that is always 5 years behind the times at all times. Lots of retirees, golf courses, horses, and all of the trappings of southern culture - rednecks, mansions, Civil War monuments and Lynyrd Skynyrd. Being a young boy in the 4th grade that didn't have a drawl, and had an interest in action-adventure, science fiction, and horror in all its forms; I was often told to get my head out of the clouds.

I liked to read (anything and everything I could get my hands on), draw, and write. I read comics, paperbacks, hardbacks, magazines, the newspaper - you name it. Of course, being in a small town outside the normal distribution routes for genre media - I didn't get to read or see *Steranko's Comixscene/ Mediascene*, *Castle of Frankenstein*, *Monster Times* and other stuff. We had *Starlog*, *Fangoria*, and *Famous Monsters* and Marvel & DC - the "mainstream." We did have a 2nd hand bookstore called **Nonesuch Books** that I used to frequent after school where I picked up ERB books, *Man from UNCLE*, and plenty of science fiction. My dad is a huge western guy so I always made sure to pick up a Zane Grey or Max Brand for him. Then he discovered the store on his own so I left him to his own devices and soon he was a *Longarm* and *Renegade* fanatic. I picked up the *Blade* books.

Above - a selection of Pulp 2.0 Press' publications to date.

Small towns like Aiken had other advantages too. There were two theaters - the Mark I & II (the family theater) and the Rocking Chair Cinema (the exploitation house) and I had fun at both. I saw the original *King Kong* at one, and *The Great Texas Dynamite Chase* at the other. If we wanted to see blockbuster movies we had to drive across the river to Augusta, Georgia. That's where I saw *Superman* and *Midway*. Bottom line, I could see just about any sort of movie - exploitation, horror, sci-fi, imports - as long as it was cheap.

I graduated high school, and went off to college at a small liberal arts college in Clinton, SC. I earned a bachelor's degree in History primarily because I loved all of the stories and characters of history. I wanted to do something with that interest, but as always that voice I heard as a kid, "Get your head out of the clouds, Bill," was in the back of my mind.

I figured I needed to do just that, so I enlisted in the USAF right out of college and had a Top Secret Security Clearance within 4 months. I was part of the 4450th TG that supported the mission of the F-117A Stealth Fighter. I was stationed (officially) in Las Vegas, NV at Nellis AFB, but spent most of every week on the Nevada test range near Area 51. So, I would fly back and forth every week - it was like I had a Vegas vacation every weekend.

This was in the mid - 80's, and small-town Bill was living in one of the entertainment meccas of the west. I went to shows, theaters - 4 near my apartment alone, two comic-book stores, and of course the newly minted entertainment business, the Video Store. I gorged myself on all of it, getting a taste of all of the stuff that I missed as a kid. I became enamored with the new business model of making movies directly for the home entertainment market. I think part of it was the lure of the VHS box art, and part of it was the idea that I could do it independently which appealed to my social anxiety.

So, after 4 years of discipline and structure, I went back to SC and went back to school. I used the G.I. Bill and got a second degree in media arts - film, video, audio, and photography. I worked hard, and crewed on indie features, commercials, industrials, and eventually bigger movies like *Die Hard With A Vengeance* which shot a ton of its scenes in SC including the great subway car crash. I worked a lot in SC, NC, and Georgia but it was always a struggle and I wasn't learning the business angles that I needed to learn in order to be able to make my own media and sell it in the marketplace.

I moved to Los Angeles. I didn't have any money. I had just broken up with my girlfriend. I really didn't know anyone there. I had a dog. All I had was a car and a dream. I know that sounds cliche', but there I was living the Hollywood cliche'. It wasn't too long before I was interviewed for a job as an assistant at Omega Entertainment and got it. I worked for the CEO, director Nico Mastorakis (*Island of Death*) doing everything he needed. I was also taking seminar courses in screenwriting, and writing my ass off. I wrote 4 scripts in four years, a ton of short stories to exercise those muscles and got to the point where I was freelancing on weekends to polish someone else's script, give notes, or consult on the production or marketing end of a project.

I moved on and got a job at York Entertainment where I dealt with independent film every day. People sent in their films, and you could tell their intentions were good, they just didn't know what it took to sell a film. So as Director of Marketing, I was responsible for working with the sales team and the boss to repackage these movies. Over a hundred or so marketing campaigns later I got pretty good at spotting trends to capitalize on, and remarket films so they could sell. We were also producing low budget pictures - approximately four films a year - to go with the 48 other films we were selling. That's right - we repackaged and sold a new film every week!

What is the background to Pulp 2.0 Press and what do you hope to achieve through it?

2008 had rolled around and suddenly the economy tanked due to the manipulation of the housing market. I was working hard, but suddenly about half of my business contacts were gone.

So, I started looking around for some way to create low cost media to share with other like-minded pulp addicts. I was developing a reputation among writing circles as the guy who reboots / restores / rethinks / repurposes older material that needed a facelift, so I started there. Part of my strategy was to search the internet and find all sorts of cool new stuff and share it with people. I wasn't alone in that many folks started sharing their interests and hobbies in new ways. If I played Pulp 2.0 right, I could bring (and have brought) new, juicy shameless entertainment to new audiences.

I first noticed you with your compilations of Donald Glut Frankenstein novels – how did they come about?

Well I was actively trying to find a book series to bring back. I wanted to do a series because if you're going to do it, set it up so you do a lot of it in a row and capitalize on it all. That sounds really capitalist of me, but the bottom line was I wanted to fill my bookshelves with books I had only heard about, or glimpsed, but never had the chance to sit down and read in a proper manner. That was my motivation.

I had picked up a bunch of the Lory **Draculas**, and the **Richard Blades**, but as I investigated the copyright holders I always hit a dead end. (The Lyle Kenyon Engel dead end if you know what I mean) Then I wanted to read the **New Adventures of Frankenstein** series by Don Glut, so I went to eBay and to get all eleven books in the condition I wanted - decent, not pristine - I would have had to spend around $300.00. I was pissed.

There was no way in this day and age of digital technology that any paperback book should be a) out of print, or b) cost $27 to read. I knew I was somehow on the right track. I just had to work harder, faster, more. I talked to some friends of Don's who I knew, and told them to have Don give me a call. Later that day, Don called me. I went through my spiel, and he asked me if I thought we could succeed. I told him I didn't know, but that I would learn and at the very least we would get the books out there.

It did take a long time, and I fell down a couple of times. We ended up releasing Don's blaxploitation vampire novel *Brother Blood* first as a way to test the waters, and learn the maze we were jumping into. Long story short, we were able to get two terrific looking, huge volumes out there that include a twelfth and final novel in the series that Don wrote specifically for the set.

Why do you think the pop culture of the 60s and 70s endures?

I think that every decade has some aspects to it that endure. The 30's had the pulp magazine covers that planted the roots for paperbacks in the 50's and beyond. The 40's had colorful movie posters and lobby cards and comic strips and comic books - all of which made their way to the 60's and 70's where they were just cocky enough to bend and break the rules. This was the decade that Marvel Comics debuted. This was the decade where Jean

Bill Cunningham (left) and Donald F Glut (right) at the launch of Pulp 2.0's publication of Brother Blood.

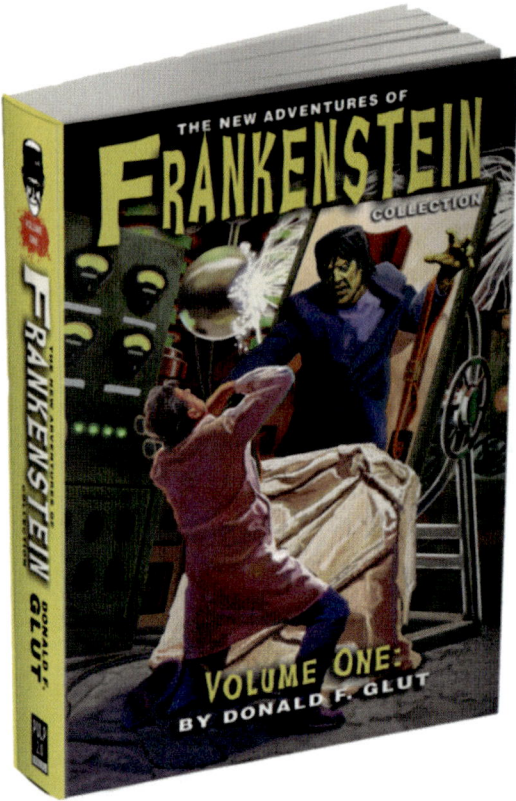

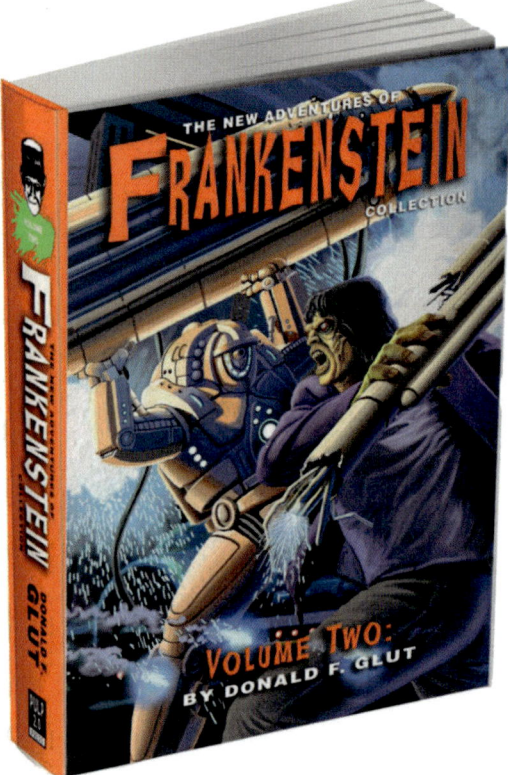

Shrimpton and David Bailey, model & photographer, brought an outsider's perspective to fashion photography and helping to usher in the whole "swinging London" vibe.

In addition, the 60's (and on into the 70's) was a time where the social boundaries were being pushed outward. You could discuss sex, politics and religion in polite company. You could craft stories that didn't have to "pass the censor." While it was much-needed, it also led to some pretty shameless activity on the part of certain publishers, movie producers and the like. They lived for pushing the boundaries because it paid the bills.

The 70's sharpened the knife a bit by giving us more and (sometimes) better hard-bitten fiction that reflected the reality. Watergate, Viet Nam, you name it. In America crime was everywhere, and we revised our policing and social order a bit to compensate - BUT - we also reflected that criminal reality in our entertainment fiction. Crime, pollution, war, corruption were all stages for conflict. The villains were no longer mad scientists from other countries - they were real villains - drug lords, prostitution rings, arms dealers, corrupt officials, serial killers, and corporate types. The old saying from the **Pogo** comic strip applies - "*I have met the enemy and he is us.*"

All of this lurid, juicy pulp fiction allowed us to deal with the realities of life. Just like in the 30's with pulp characters, we could point to **The Destroyer**, **The Executioner**, **The Butcher** or **The Marksman** and say, "They're out there protecting us, doing what they have to do to save society." It didn't hurt that this fantasy was wrapped in colorful covers that sold action and sex.

Tell me more about the Killer comic book series you are translating.

I have recently written a film book *Death Kiss: The Book of the Movie* about the

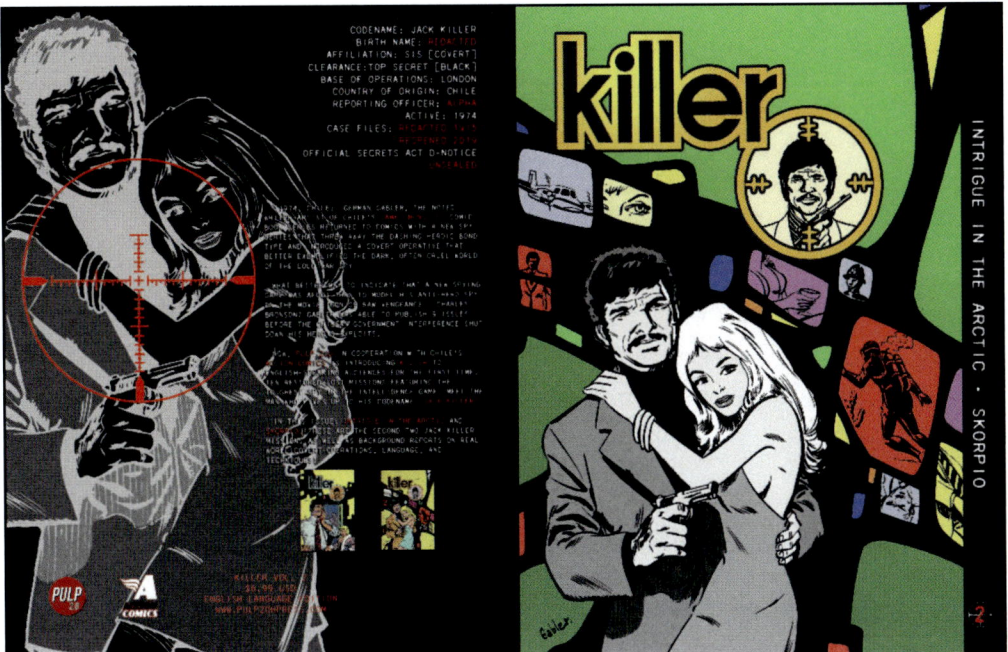

Above - volume two of the five-issue programme from Pulp 2.0 to reprint Killer, the Chilean espionage strip featuring a Charles 'Death Wish' Bronson look-a-like.

production of a low budget vigilante exploitation movie starring Robert Kovacs Bronzi who bears an uncanny resemblance to Charles Bronson. So, for the book I was doing a lot of visual-related Bronson research, and came across this image of a cheaply printed comic book cover with Bronson's image on it titled *Killer*.

From there it was a matter of contacting the Claudio Alvarez who was acting as the agent for Germán Gabler, *Killer*'s creator. I learned all about how Gabler was forced out of the Chilean comic industry due to the dictatorship taking over the media and telling him he couldn't produce the *James Bond 007* comics anymore. He took a year off and worked elsewhere, then when things calmed down he came back to Chile's comics industry with *Killer*.

The comic is very much a product of its time. 1974 was right in the middle of the Cold War. Crime was on the rise, and as I said before that was very much reflected in our fiction - not only in America, but around the world. We were exporting our movies, TV and books around the planet, and one of our pulpiest exports was an action movie called *The Mechanic* starring Charles Bronson. Gabler took Bronson as his model and created *Killer* around James Bondian spy antics and Bronson crime busting.

Claudio and his team were remastering the artwork, and providing me with the base translation. I am rewriting the dialogue to give it a more natural feel to English speaking ears, and adding touches of intelligence community terminology. If you're a fan of Bond, Callan, Harry Palmer, or George Smiley then you're going to feel right at home with Jack Killer. In addition, it's a peek into how comics were designed back in 1970's Chile - a straight forward plot (or so you think), violence, off-camera sex, a bit of nudity, all wrapped in a load of spy atmosphere. It's a comic that English readers have never seen before, but they'll recognize if for no other reason than the comic "stars Charles Bronson."

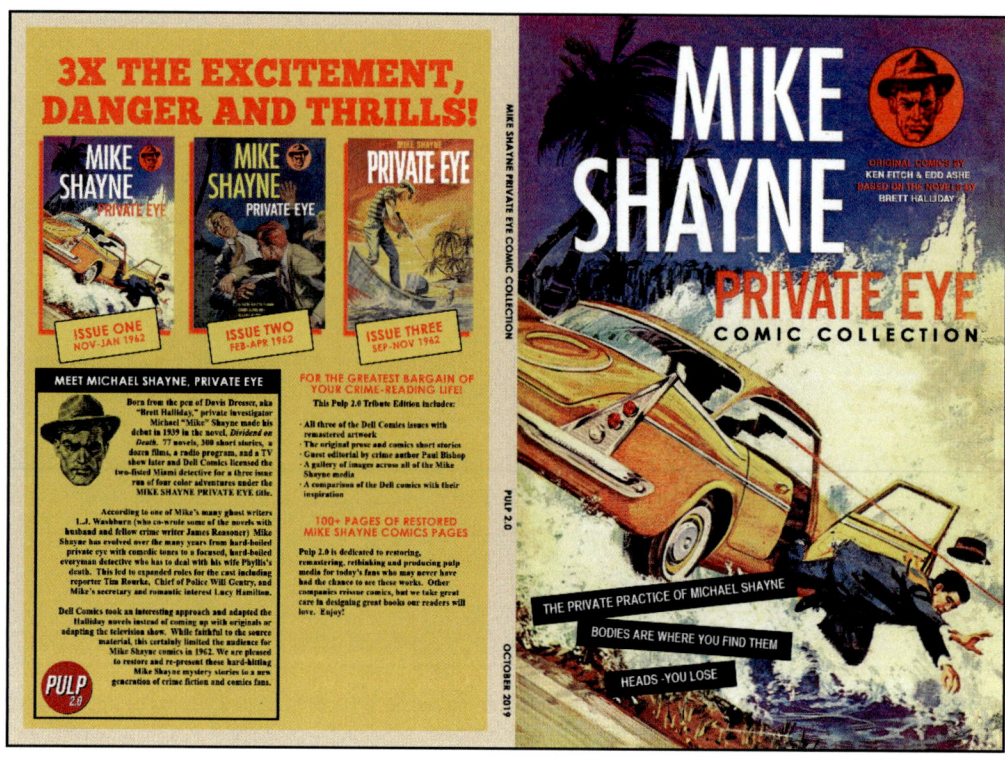

Above - a collection of three rare comic book adaptations of Mike Shayne currently being prepared by Bill and his Pulp 2.0 Press.

I've also seen that you've announced a series of Mike Shayne comics. What can you tell us about these.

Mike has a long history of many novels, many issues of his digest magazine, a long-running radio show, a movie series, and a television show... and a three issue run of comics. Huh?! In reading the books, I realized it was because the comics were very faithful to the novels - these were comic *adaptations*! I had my next tribute collection...

So Mike is one of those books where I am going to take my time with. I'm doing a few pages at a time and assembling everything in November. Paul Bishop (*The Fay Croaker series*) has added an introductory essay and I'm putting together a gallery of images from the Mike Shayne movies and TV show. I think it's a great introduction to Mike Shayne, and to what we want to do with our tribute books.

I think self-publishing can be very rewarding but also lonely and frustrating. What have been the ups and downs for you to date?

There are several ups and downs as there are with all opportunities, but for creative people I think one of the biggest things is when you put all of your energy into a book (or film or comic) and it doesn't sell. I love the process, and the final product. I love that I am able, by myself if necessary, to write, design and publish a book by myself. But that sting when people don't buy your book, or don't even take the time to write 4-5 sentences as a review on Amazon -- that's all a special sort of pain.

The highs are when you see people giving one of our books to someone as a gift, or in the case of a comic, to their kids. People who write reviews on Amazon for us are angels - even a bad review is helpful.

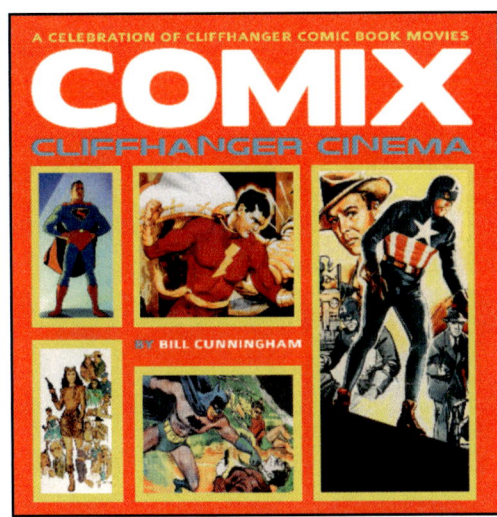

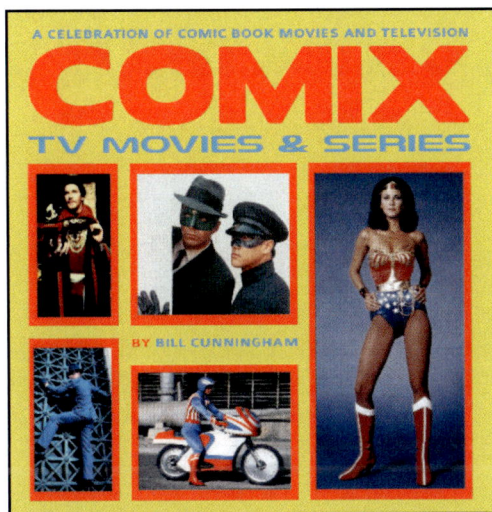

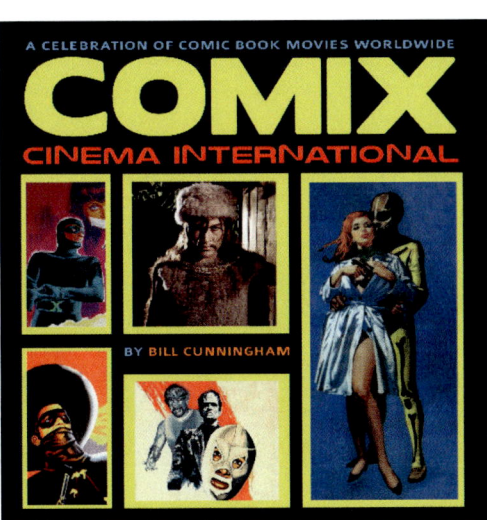

What's next for Pulp 2.0?

We are currently in pre-order for *The Killer Collection* (all five volumes for the price of four), and for *Celluloid Wars: Battle Beyond The Stars* which is a book in our *Cinexploits!* line of film books. *Killer: Volumes 1 and 2* are both currently on sale on Amazon with the next three available by Christmas.

Mike Shayne, Private Eye should be available at the end of November.

Automatons: The Book of the Movie will be available soon. The Director, James Felix McKenney is reviewing it for edits.

Joan Boix's Terror Comics is currently being translated. These are Spanish language comics that are similar to Warren's Creepy, Eerie, and so on… He's adapted Poe and Lovecraft. It'll debut in 2020.

My two big projects for 2020 are the three-volume *Comix Cinema* series that celebrates comic book movies and TV series from all around the world; and *Lethal Ladies Volume 1* which covers the four book series *The Dark Angel*. I also have a book series that I am republishing that incorporates material from several sources. If you're an old school science fiction adventure kid like I am, then you'll be happy.

I might be wrong, but I have you down as more of a comics guy than a paperbacks guy. Anything you want to say in your defence before sentencing?

You are so wrong. It is far worse than you ever imagined.
I'm a comics guy.
I'm a paperbacks guy.
I'm a movie and television guy.
I'm an Old Time Radio guy.
I'm a cartoons guy.
I'm a toy guy.
Because, to me, it's all the same. It's all pulp. Pulp is not a medium, it's an Extra Large.

ANDREW NETTE co-editor of the successful Girl Gangs, Biker Boys and Cool Cats, talks to The Fanatic about the follow-up volume.

STICKING IT TO THE MAN

How was *Girl Gangs, Biker Boys and Real Cool Cats* received, and how did it turn out compared to your own hopes?

Iain McIntyre, my co-editor on *Girl Gangs, Biker Boys and Real Cool Cats*, and I were thrilled with what out publisher, PM Press, did with the book. The layout and editorial work were first rate, which is something quite a few people commented on. Everyone who read it seemed to have really dug it, which is great.

To be completely honest, not only did this book and its sequel, *Sticking it to the Man: Revolution and Counterculture in Pulp and Popular Fiction, 1950-1980*, take a huge amount of work on the part of ourselves and the people who contributed, they were expensive for the publisher to put out. Like all authors, I'd like these books to reach a bigger market, and I am hoping that people who read *Sticking it to the Man* will discover and buy *Girl Gangs, Biker Boys and Real Cool Cats*.

What can you tell us about this new volume? *Sticking it to the Man*

Sticking it to the Man examines the depiction of revolutionary movements and the counterculture in pulp and popular fiction in the US, UK and Australia from 1950 to 1960. It runs the gamut of movements and causes, from civil rights and the rise of black power, workers movements, and gay and lesbian liberation, to anti-war – particularly anti-Vietnam War – and feminism. While the focus remains on pulp paperbacks, we range a little further in the second book in that we have deliberately included some fiction which fits more into the definition of popular mainstream paperback fiction; work like Judith Rossner's 1975 book, *Looking For Mister Goodbar*, some of the gay and lesbian fiction, and some of the books that explores race and class in the UK.

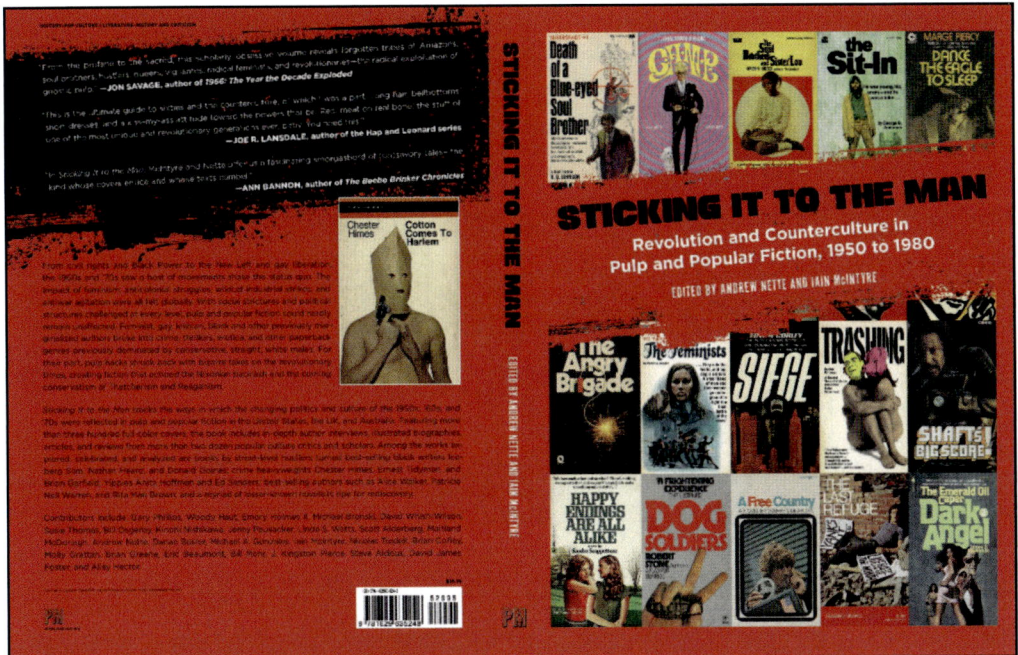

Above - the newly published Sticking it to the Man is 336 pages and full-colour. It's available through the website pmpress.org

That said, the line between pulp and popular mainstream fiction is a very blurred one. A lot of books that are considered 'pulp' were first released in hard back format, often by very prestigious publishers, and where subsequently re-released in more luridly packaged paperback format.

Of course, you can never cover off on everything. Even now, nearly a couple of years after Iain and I sent the book to the publisher, I am still stumbling across books and authors I would have liked to include but, alas, there is simply not the room to do everything. But I think we have a pretty good spread. The important thing from my perspective is that Sticking it the Man, like Girl Gangs, Biker Boys and Real Cool Cats, has a good mix of the titles you might expect to see, alongside work from far lesser known, sometimes completely forgotten authors. Indeed, Sticking it the Man contains more material that is far less known than a lot of the youth pulp that we featured in the first book.

I really welcomed the coverage of African-American authors, and not just Iceberg Slim, Robert Beck and Chester Himes, but the likes of Jospeh Nazel. How did you encounter these authors' works yourself and how did the focus in the book come about?

The inclusion of these black authors was just an obvious place for the book to go. As social and economic structures gradually started to change in the post war period, especially into the 1960s, and various left, progressive and revolutionary movements gained momentum, pulp and popular fiction changed as well. Feminist, gay, lesbian and black writers broke into publishing in larger numbers.

Obviously, a lot of people have heard of the crime writer, Chester Himes. But he is just one of a large number of black authors who started penning pulp and popular fiction, particularly in the 1960s. I was aware of a lot of these writers, particularly those that worked for the prolific 'black experience' LA based pulp publisher (which was actually white

Andrew - The blaxploitation style cover for number seven in the Holloway House series featuring character known as 'the Iceman'.

Andrew - Robert Beck's Pimp was an incredibly influential pulp novel. This is a very rare copy of the first 1967 printing of the story by Holloway House.

owned), Holloway House: Donald Goines, Joe Nazel and Robert Beck aka Iceberg Slim. But there are a number of others I wasn't familiar with, like Ronald Fair and Nathan Heard, to name just two.

These black writers ran the gamut from pulp hacks, who were happy to churn out salacious crime stories to earn a pay check, to more serious, almost semi-literary authors. But, whatever their style and content, all of them were writing about the black experience in 1960s and 1970s America, including the poverty and racism experienced by black communities, and various responses to it, like the rise of civil rights movement and far more militant movements like the Black Panthers. We were also lucky enough to have people like crime writer Gary Phillips and academic Kinohi Nashikawa who were knowledgeable about some of these less known writers and prepared to write great pieces for us (and, by the way, if people want to know more about Holloway House, check out Kinohi's terrific book on the subject, *Street Players*)

There seemed more of an Australian flavour to this volume in terms of not necessarily Australian books following American trends, but dealing with themes and issues very specific to Australia such as the portrayal of native Aborigines. Was this intentional?

Definitely intentional. Australia had a far smaller publishing marketplace and, hence, the volume of pulp and popular

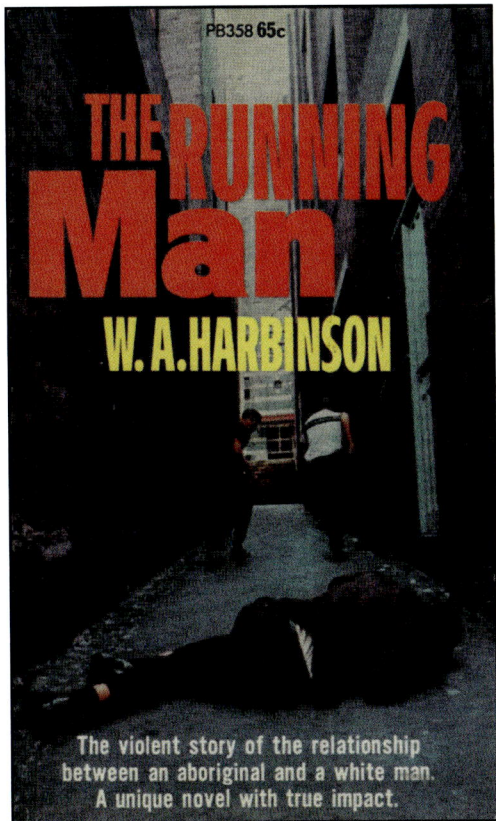

Andrew - The Running Man is one of several novels examined in Sticking it to the Man: Revolution and Counterculture, 1950-1980, dealing with Indigenous Australians.

Andrew - I love the cover of this 1973 novel, better described as experimental fiction than pulp, about the real life small, far left urban guerrilla group active in Britain in the 1970s.

fiction was published in the 1950s and 1960s, in particular, was less than was the case in larger markets such as the US and UK. That's just the reality. That said, we want to make sure Australia, where we are both from, is not forgotten.

I wasn't expecting men's adventure fiction such as Lone Wolf to be covered. How did they fit in to the books theme of counterculture and rebellion?

When Iain and I originally discussed *Sticking it to the Man*, we wanted to include material that fell under the heading of books that were, consciously or not, a literary/publishing backlash to the radical and countercultural fiction that was published in the second half of the 1960s and the early 1970s. This includes all the vigilante pulp dealing with cops and private citizens who decide they have had enough of inner-city crime, of which Brian Garfield's 1972 book, *Death Wish*, is probably the best known, as well as the various series featuring Vietnam veterans taking on all manner of local and global threats.

I love this stuff and read quite a bit of it for the book. But in the end, we had to trim the contents and some of this had to go. That said, there is a great piece on vigilante pulp, which focuses on *Death Wish*, the Dirty Harry books and David Morrell's 1972 thriller, *First Blood*, which became the inspiration for the series of films starring Sylvester Stallone. As you say, there is also a piece on the vigilante series featuring a Vietnam vet ex-cop by Mike Barry, aka the science fiction writer, Barry Malzberg, penned by yours truly. Malzberg wrote some incredibly penetrating and thought-provoking science fiction. But he was not above writing whatever publishers asked him to, like the Lone Wolf series, the over ten books in which he belted out in a couple of years. This series is quite fascinating. Not only is the character, Burt Wulff, quite literally insane (and Malzberg consciously wrote him this way); his battle against a shadowy drug dealing criminal organisation is very obviously a stand in for the failed war in Vietnam.

You touched on gay pulp literature, which strikes me a subject which warrants a whole volume to itself. I think these books were important when pretty much any other media was devoid of gay characters. What's your take on this branch of pulp fiction?

There is so much that could be said about lesbian and gay pulp fiction, it is hard to know where to start. Let's just say, there was a lot of it, and, like the books produced by the black writers I mentioned earlier, even the trashiest, more salacious examples of it, are important given they appeared in a time when there were very few, overt representations of lesbian and gay experience in popular culture. *Sticking it to the Man* has over half a dozen features, interviews and reviews related to these books. This work holds up a fascinating and important mirror to the

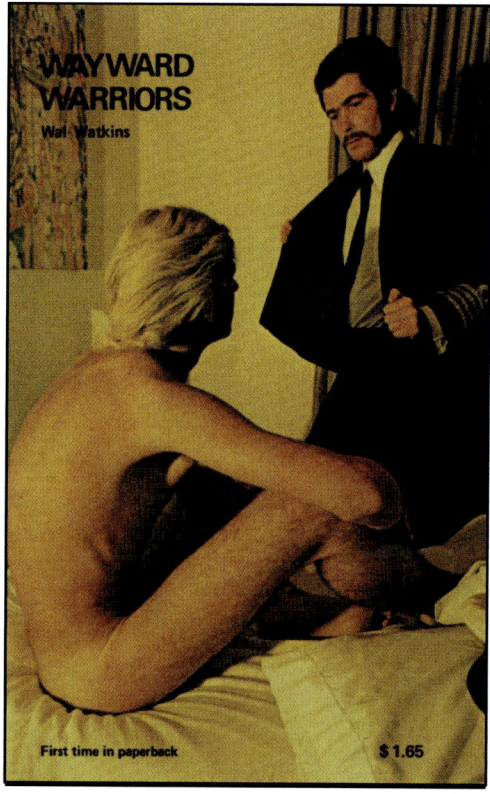

Andrew - Released by the short-lived Australian publisher of pulp and popular fiction, Gold Star Publications, Wayward Warriors was about homosexuality in the Australian navy. The cover, deliberately chosen by the publisher for its sexually suggestive nature, ensured it was one of the publisher's best selling titles.

Andrew - Parley J Cooper's The Feminists is one of a large number of pulp novels featured that appeared in the US in response to the rising influence of second wave feminism.

experience and treatment of these communities in Australia, the US and the UK.

It was great to see a chapter on my beloved New English Library and their sexploitation works. How often were you encountering these books yourself in Australia and what impact did they have on you?

I share your love for the wonder that was 1970s NEL pulp. There was, quite literally no social trend, no then current event, that NEL could not turn into lurid pulp thrills, including feminism and the left student movement against the Vietnam War. NEL books, and their earlier variants, Four Square, were remaindered in large numbers in Australia. I still find them every now and again in opportunity shops and second-hand books stores, but less and less, I am afraid. The exception are NEL's so-called 'slaver' or 'plantation pulps', which still turn up in large numbers. Presumably this is because their subject matter is so out of sync with contemporary sensibilities, that the owners just want to get rid of them.

What do you plan next? A third volume?

Yes. Originally, *Sticking it to the Man* contained quite a lot of material covering radical science fiction. But, as I mentioned earlier, the book was getting out of hand lengthwise, and we had to cut some material. Plus we realised that radical science was potentially a book in itself, which is what we proposed to our publisher,

Andrew - Trashing is a fiction take on Yippies, written by Ann Fettamen, a pseudonym for Anita Hoffman, wife of Yippie leader, Abbie Hoffman.

Andrew - I love cover design and the cover blurb of this crime novel set amidst the American student protests of the late 1960s.

PM Press. They agreed and we are currently working on a third book in the series, on radical science fiction. It is tentatively titled, *Dangerous Visions and New Worlds: Radical Science Fiction, 1950-1980*. We have some great content for this and are playing around with presenting the material, especially all the amazing covers, in a slightly different way to *Sticking it to the Man* and *Girl Gangs, Biker Boys and Real Cool Cats*.

And finally, I know you as a crime writer and as the next issue of The Paperback Fanatic is a Gold Medal special, I wondered what your take on Gold Medal and its authors might be.

That's exciting. As I am sure your issue will discuss, Gold Medal was an incredibly important series in the history of the mass paperback in the US. It helped popularise the spread of original pulp paperback fiction, as opposed to softcover paperback editions of works that had previously appeared in hard back, which is what a lot of paperback fiction had been until Gold Medal came on the scene. Plus, in addition to the covers, a lot of the stories were terrific and really stand the test of time. Anyone who disagrees should go and read the 1953 the amazingly good Gold Medal crime novel, *Black Wings Has My Angel*, by Elliot Chaze, and that is just one example.

Andrew - One of the many examples of gay Young Adult covered in Sticking it to the Man: Revolution and Counterculture, 1950-1980.

Andrew - While Vietnam and its aftermath were the backdrop of numerous pulp and popular novels, books actually set in Vietnam were very rare until the 1980s. Con Sellers' Where Have All the Soldiers Gone, published in 1969, is an exception.

Made in the USA
Monee, IL
17 February 2020